Southwest Oxford and Norwich Townships Ontario in Colour Photos, Saving Our History One Photo at a Time

Photography by Barbara Raué
©2019

Series Name: Cruising Ontario

Book 241: Southwest Oxford and part of Norwich Townships

Cover photo: 431 Main Street, Springford, Page 67

©All the photos in this book have been taken with my cameras. I own the rights to them.

Series Name: Cruising Ontario, Saving Our History One Photo at a Time in colour photos

Books Available in Alphabetical Order:
Aberfoyle, Acton, Ajax, Alton, Amherstburg, Ancaster, Arthur, Auburn, Aylmer, Ayr, Beaver Valley, Belfountain, Belgrave, Belleville, Bloomingdale, Blyth, Brantford, Brockville, Burford, Burlington, Caledon, Caledonia, Cambridge, Carlow, Cayuga, Chatsworth, Cheltenham, Clifford, Colborne, Collingwood, Conestogo, Delhi, Dorchester to Aylmer, Drayton, Drumbo, Dundas, Dunlop, Dunnville, Eden Mills, Elmira, Elora, Embro, Erin, Essex, Fergus, Fort Erie, Georgetown, Goderich, Grimsby, Guelph, Hagersville, Haldimand County, Hamilton, Hanover, Harriston, Hespeler, Ingersoll, Inglewood, Innerkip, Jarvis, Kingston, Kingsville, Kitchener, Lake Superior, Lincoln, Linwood, Listowel, London, Lucknow, Merrickville, Mono, Mount Brydges, Mount Forest, Mount Pleasant, Neustadt, New Hamburg, Newboro, Newport, Niagara-on-the-Lake, Niagara Falls, North Bay, Oakville, Onondaga, Orangeville, Orillia, Oshawa, Otterville, Owen Sound, Palmerston, Paris, Parry Sound, Pelham, Perth, Peterborough, Petrolia, Pickering, Port Colborne, Port Elgin, Port Hope, Port Perry, Portland, Preston, Rockwood, Sarnia, Sault Ste. Marie, Seaforth, Sheffield, Shelburne, Simcoe, Smiths Falls, Smithville, Southampton, St. Catharines, St. George, St. Jacobs, St. Marys, St. Thomas, Stoney Creek, Stouffville, Stratford, Strathroy, Sudbury, Tavistock, Terra Cotta, Thamesford, Thunder Bay, Tillsonburg, Toronto, Uxbridge, Waterdown, Waterford, Waterloo, Welland, Wellesley, West Flamborough, Westport, Whitby, Windsor, Wingham, Woodstock, York

Book 238-239: Ingersoll
Book 240: Zorra Township
Book 241: Southwest Oxford

Table of Contents

Southwest Oxford Township
Sweaburg   Page 9

Foldens   Page 13

Salford   Page 17

Ostrander   Page 19

Verschoyle   Page 20

Culloden   Page 22

Brownsville   Page 23

Delmer   Page 29

Beachville   Page 34

Norwich Township
Oxford Centre   Page 49

Curries   Page 57

Springford   Page 60

Milldale   Page 68

South-West Oxford is a township in Ontario in Oxford County. A predominantly rural municipality, South-West Oxford was formed in 1975 through the amalgamation of Dereham and West Oxford townships and the village of Beachville.

South-West Oxford extends north to south from the middle of Oxford County along the Thames River/Highway 401/Woodstock-Ingersoll east-west corridor to the southern boundary of the county along the Delhi-Tillsonburg-Aylmer/Ontario Highway 3 east-west corridor. The northern boundary follows the course of the Thames River except where carveouts have extended the boundaries of Ingersoll and Woodstock into former township lands.

In its wilderness state, the former Dereham township had thousands of acres of swamp and marsh land which limited its use for agriculture. Several large drainage projects brought great improvement and remain as essential parts of the township's farmland infrastructure. The township topography still has several large forested areas which are remnants of the original swamps on which drainage system runoff is concentrated.

At its north end, the township is underlain with an unusually pure limestone deposit centered between Ingersoll and Beachville that extends north-west through most of Zorra and south-east into Norwich. Open-pit mining of the limestone and kiln-firing to produce lime has been underway along the Thames River since pioneer days, and since the 1950s heavy industrial operations have led to nearly three thousand acres being licensed for extraction from pits more than 100 feet deep. The size of the limestone deposits is sufficient to support these operations for another century or more.

South-West Oxford includes lands in the former West Oxford township which were the earliest to be settled in Oxford County and also lands in the former Dereham township which were the last in the county to be settled. The greatest cause for slow growth in Dereham was the provincial government's decision in 1799 to auction off all the wilderness land in the township in large blocks, which thereby fell into the hands of speculators who held the land dormant for decades.

The township of South-West Oxford comprises a number of villages and hamlets, including the following communities such as *Beachville, Brownsville, Brownsville Station, Centreville, Culloden, Delmer, Dereham Centre, Foldens, Hagles Corners, Mount Elgin, Ostrander, Salford, Sweaburg, Verschoyle and Zenda.

Salford is a small village along Highway 19; it is surrounded by agricultural land and the Oxford landfill to the east. There are two churches, and the Salford Community Centre with a ball diamond.

Sweaburg is located five kilometers southwest of Woodstock. Its main intersection is Sweaburg Road and Dodge Line (County Roads 12 and 41). It had a public school for students up to grade three until 2009, and currently has Sweaburg United Church and cemetery, a ball diamond, and a convenience store.

The Township of Norwich is a located in Oxford County in southwestern Ontario. Oxford County Road 59 is the major north-south highway through much of the township. The local economy is largely agricultural, based on corn, soybean, and wheat production with dairy farming in the north part of the township and tobacco, vegetable, and ginseng farming to the south. Slowly, ginseng and traditional cash crops are replacing the former cash crop - tobacco, as demand shrinks.

Upon his arrival in the province in 1792, the first proclamation issued by John Graves Simcoe, the Lieutenant Governor of Upper Canada while still at Kingston, announced the names and boundaries he had decided upon as political boundaries for Upper Canada. For areas lying to the west of Kingston, he decided that county names would be a "mirror of Britain". To accomplish this, the sequence of names for counties along Lake Ontario became Northumberland, Durham, York and Lincoln, and for counties along Lake Erie, the names became Norfolk, Suffolk, Essex and Kent. (This was the same sequence of county names in place along the eastern seacoast of England, running from the Scottish boundary down to the English Channel.) The proclamation defined the northern boundary of Norfolk County as being the Thames River. Norwich and Dereham townships were originally within the land area designated as belonging to Norfolk County in Upper Canada, and were named after the towns of Norwich and Dereham in Norfolk County in England.

Governor Simcoe with several other government officers, guided by a party of Six Nations warriors, conducted a wilderness tour on foot up the length of the Thames River in 1793 and decided to assign additional place names to mirror those they knew along the Thames River in England. Middlesex County was the name assigned to the area around a town site reserved at the "lower forks" in the river, to be called London; Dorchester was the name for a town site at the "middle forks", and the area around the "upper forks" was to be Oxford - the same sequence of names as found along the Thames in England. When legislation was passed in Upper Canada in 1798 to implement these new divisions, Norwich and Dereham were separated from Norfolk County and added to the new Oxford County, which included also Burford, Blenheim, Blandford and Oxford townships - names drawn from Oxfordshire in England.

Shortly after returning from this tour, in March 1793, Simcoe received a petition from Thomas Ingersoll and associates asking for grant of a township to which they promised to bring settlers from New England. The group was granted the township of Oxford-on-the-Thames. In order to bring settlers into the wilderness area township, a road had to be built from Brantford up to the Thames River, a distance of thirty miles (forty-eight kilometres), and Thomas Ingersoll arranged that work over the course of the next two years. The first ones to become permanently settled in the township were likely Samuel Canfield Sr. and his wife and sons, who agreed to make their new home into a half-way stopping point for travellers along the road, at what became known as Oxford Centre.

Beachville was the heart of Oxford County with settlement beginning in 1791.

The Bostwicks, Ingersolls and Canfields were New England families who had made their start in the New World in the 1600s, and frontier living had been second nature to them for generations.

Settlement in the former Norwich Township came more than fifteen years after Oxford Township. The Norwich settlement was founded by two men: Peter Lossing and Peter De Long. Both men were from New York. Peter Lossing's house was the first one in Norwich. It now stands by the old Quaker Meeting House. Both men where Quakers. The town of Norwich began as a completely Quaker settlement.

In 1799, the Township of Norwich was laid out by surveyor William Hambly into lines and concessions and 200-acre lots. The township was divided into North and South Norwich Townships in 1855.

In 1975, Oxford County underwent countywide municipal restructuring. The Village of Norwich and the Townships of East Oxford, North Norwich and South Norwich were amalgamated to create the Township of Norwich.

Norwich includes the communities of Beaconsfield, Bond's Corners, Brown's Corners, Burgessville, Cornell, Creditville, Curries, Eastwood, Hawtrey, Hink's Corners, Holbrook, Milldale, Muir, Newark, New Durham, Norwich, Oriel, Otterville, Oxford Centre, Rock's Mills, Rosanna, Springford, Summerville, Blows, and Vandecar.

Southwest Oxford Township - Sweaburg

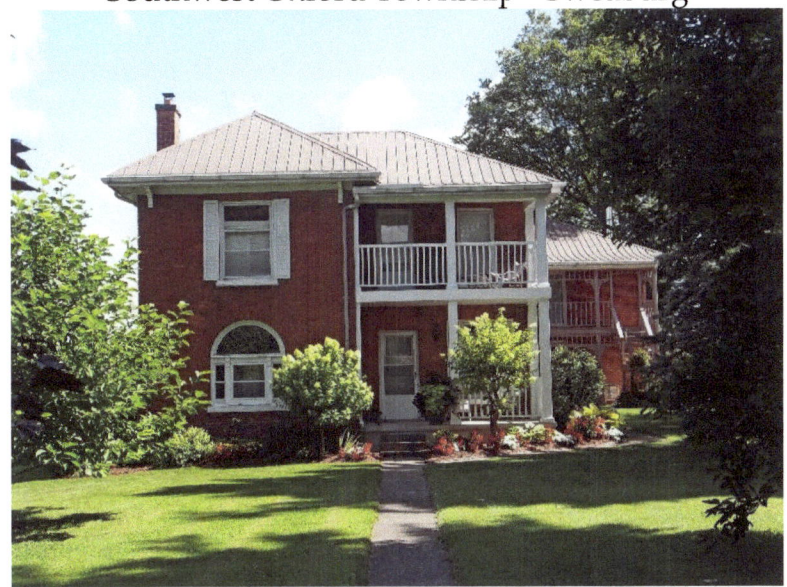

474378 Dodge Line

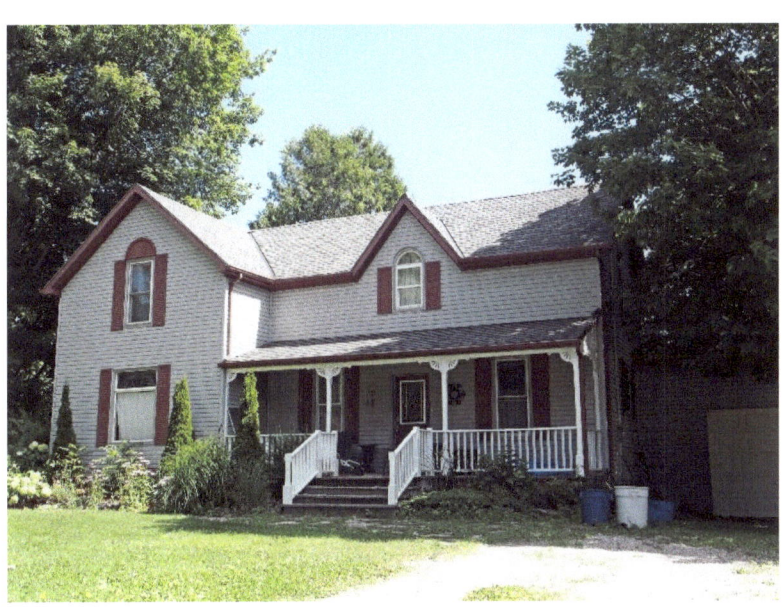

474418 Dodge Line – Gothic Revival

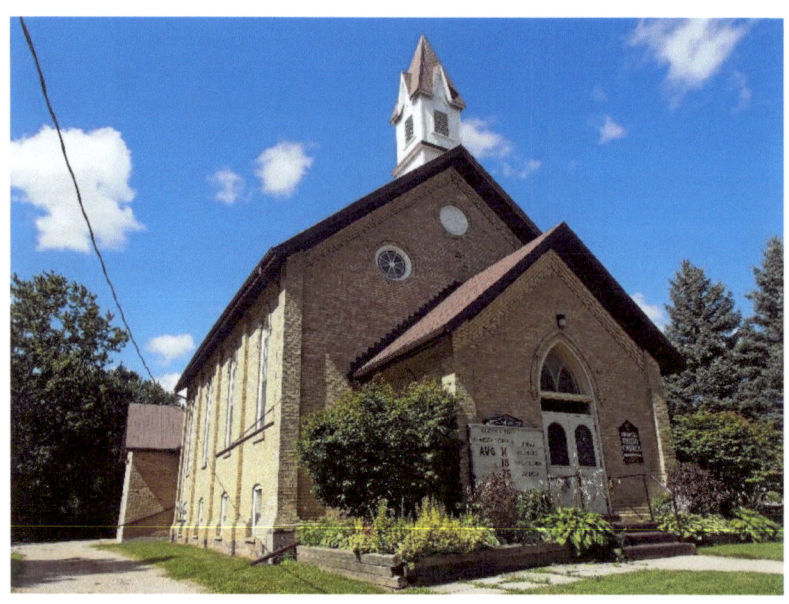

474425 Dodge Line – Sweaburg United Church - 1888 – rose window, cupola

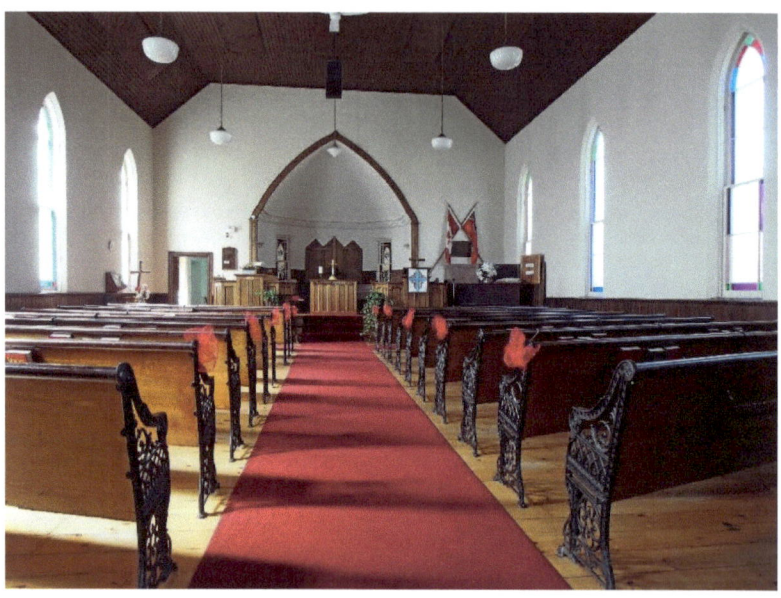

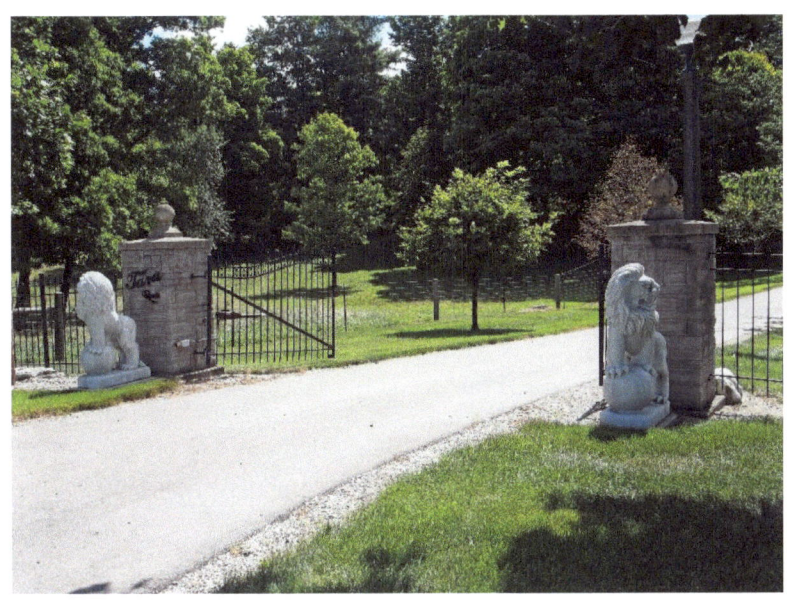

484526 Sweaburg Road

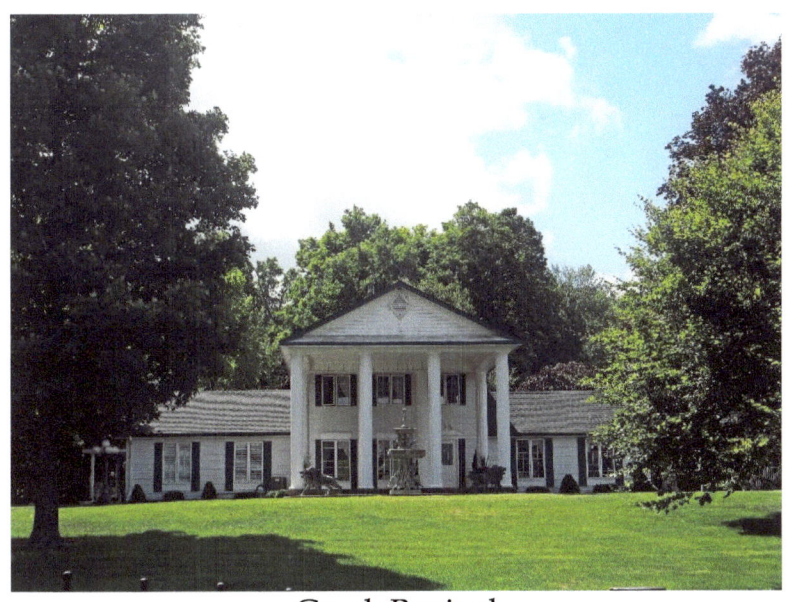

Greek Revival

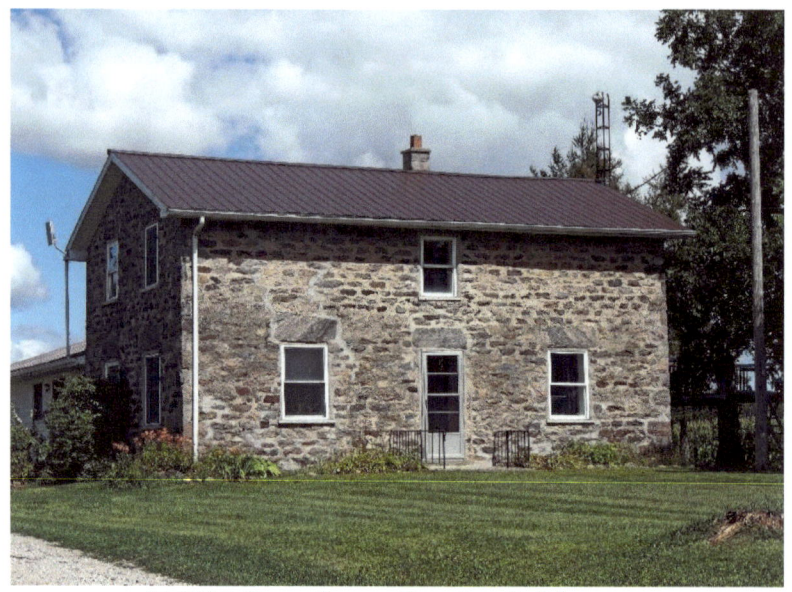

484351 Sweaburg Road – field stone

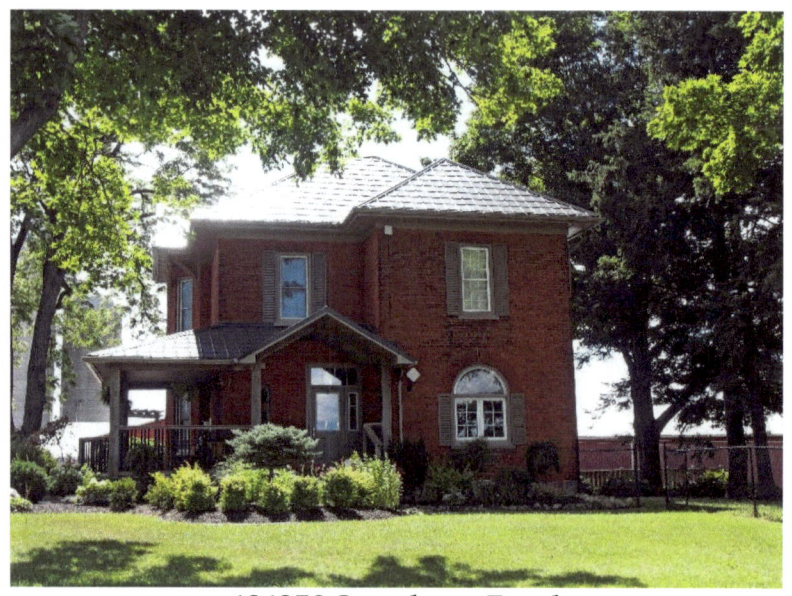

484350 Sweaburg Road

Foldens

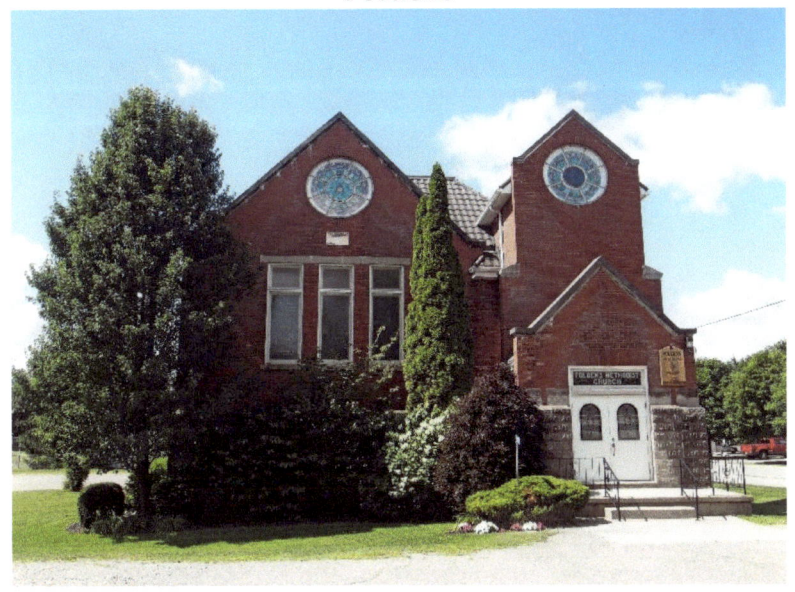

374097 Foldens Line – Foldens (Methodist) United Church – A.D. 1911 – rose windows

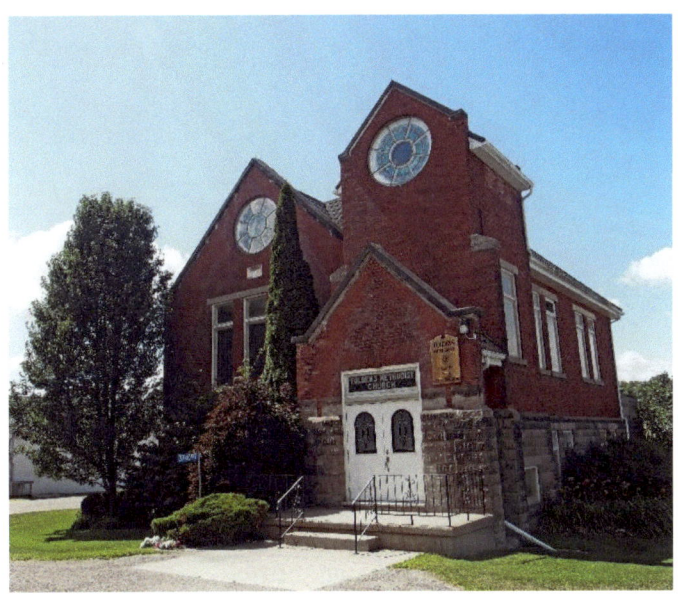

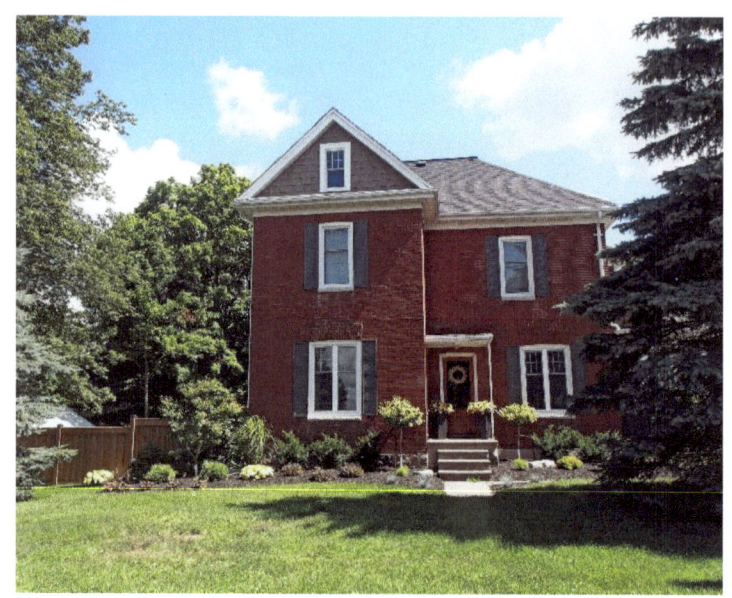
374110 Foldens Line

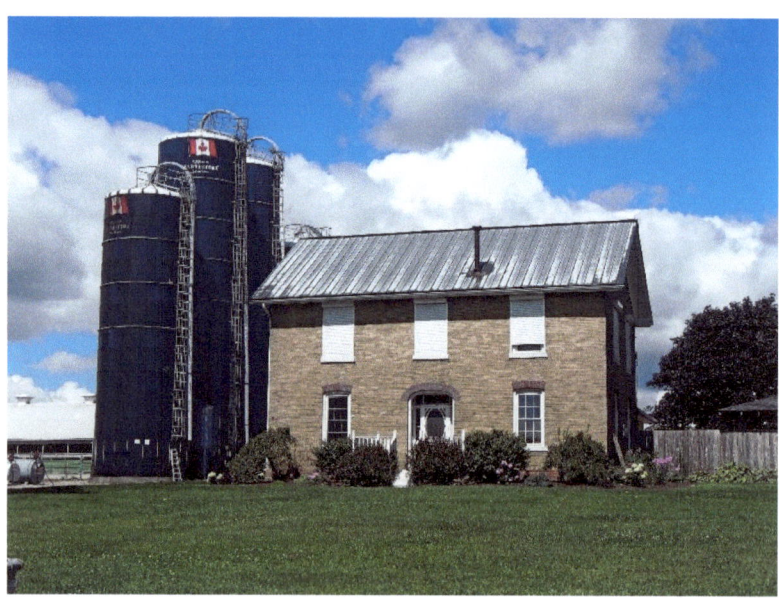
Foldens Line

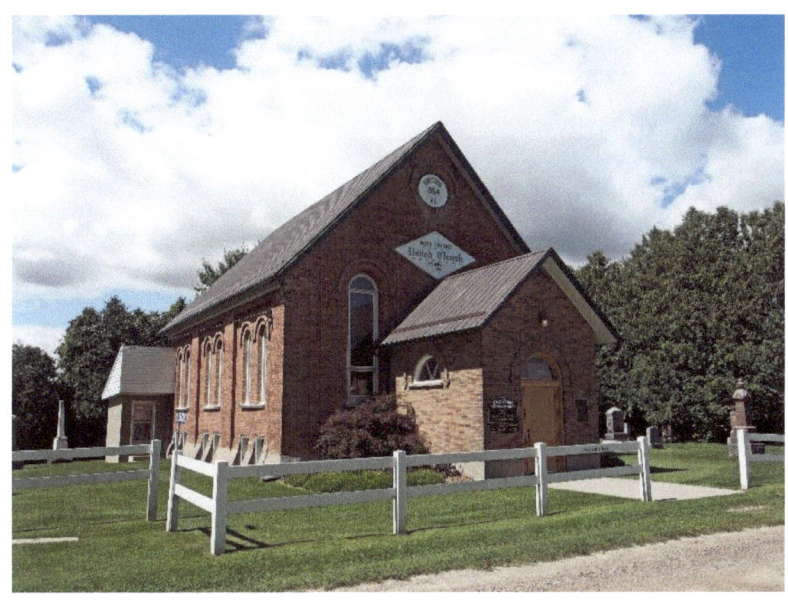

354395 Church Line West Oxford United Church – Oxford County's oldest Protestant congregation giving continuous service since its founding in 1804

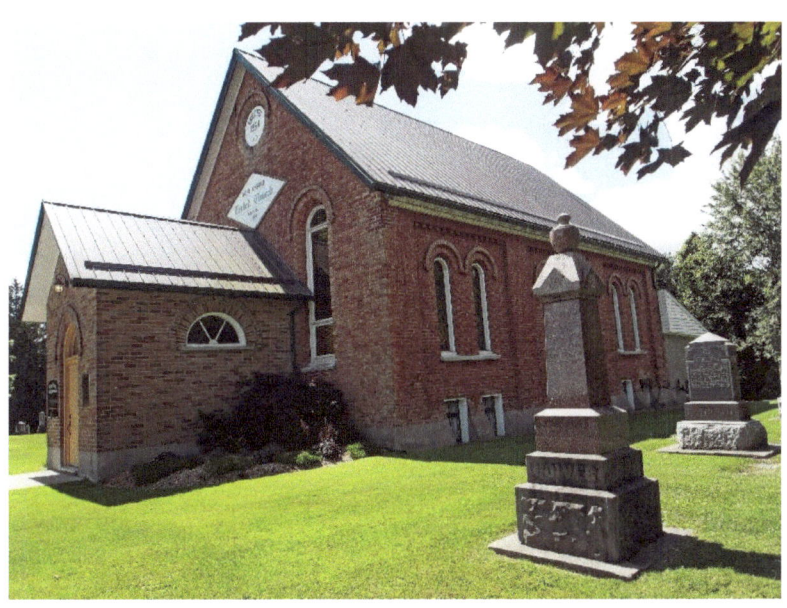

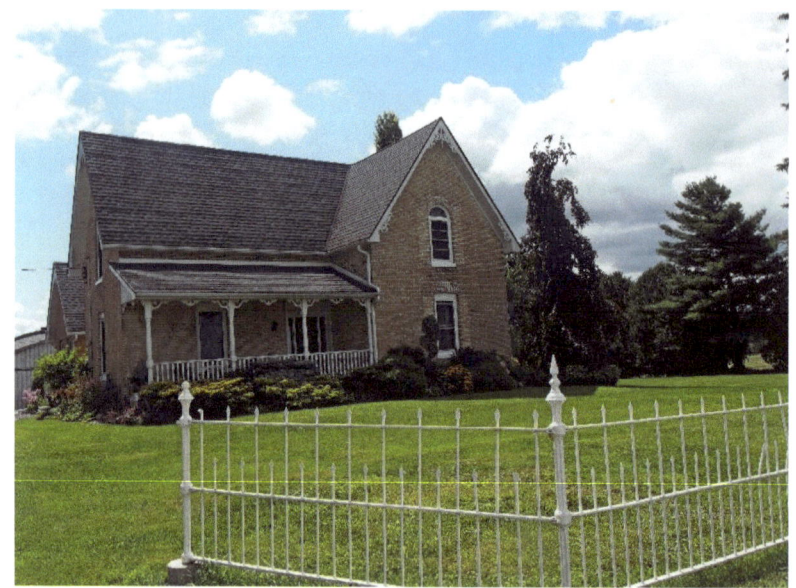
543976 Church Line – Gothic – verge board trim on gables

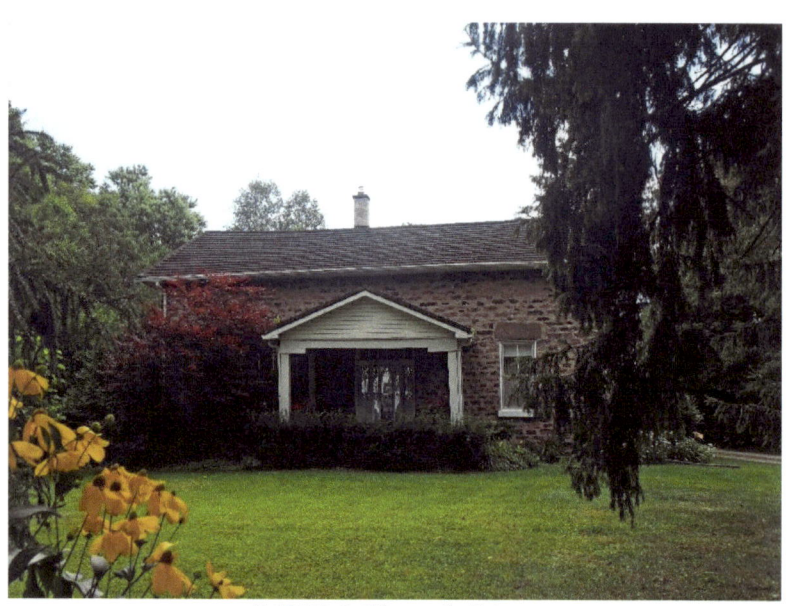
543926 Church Line

Salford

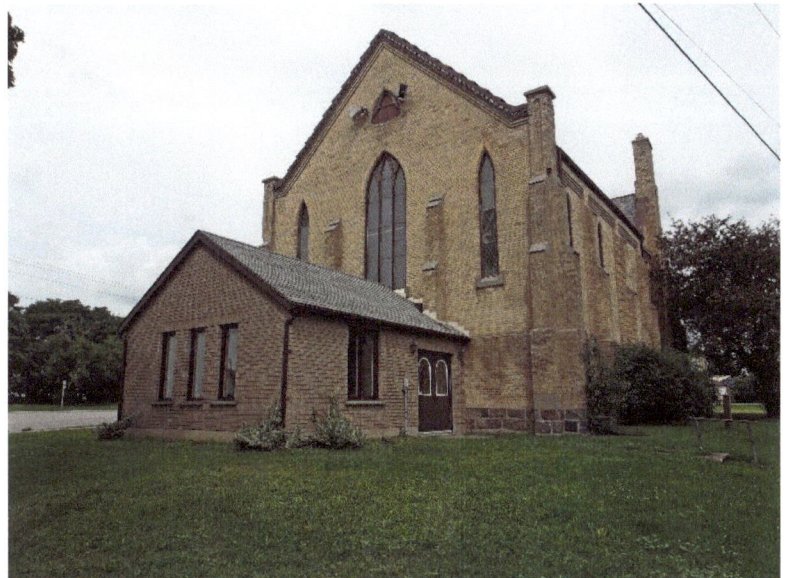

333749 Plank Line - Salford United Church – Methodist A.D. 1880 – Gothic Revival – lancet windows, buttresses

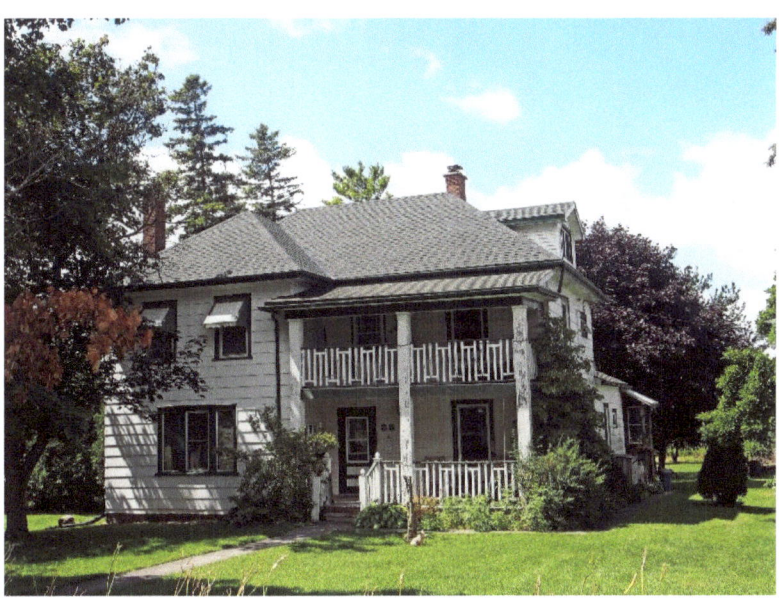

313733 Dereham Line

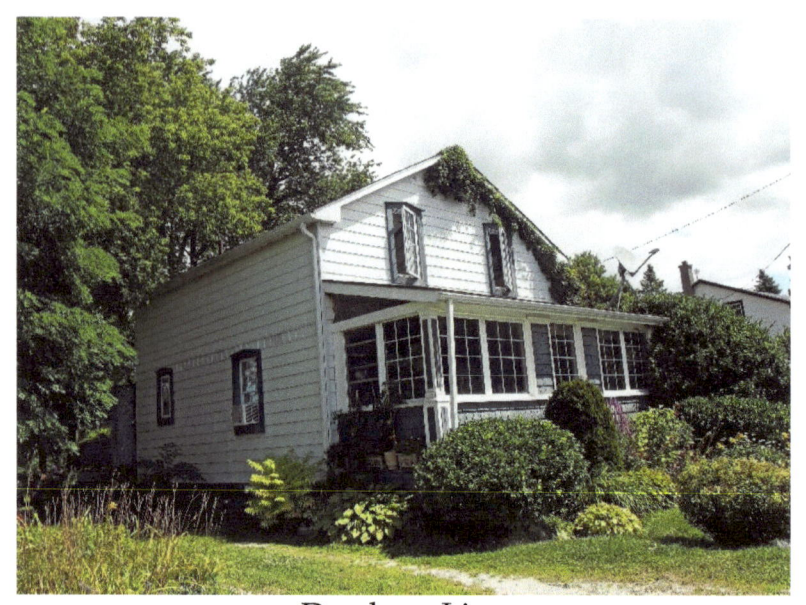

Dereham Line

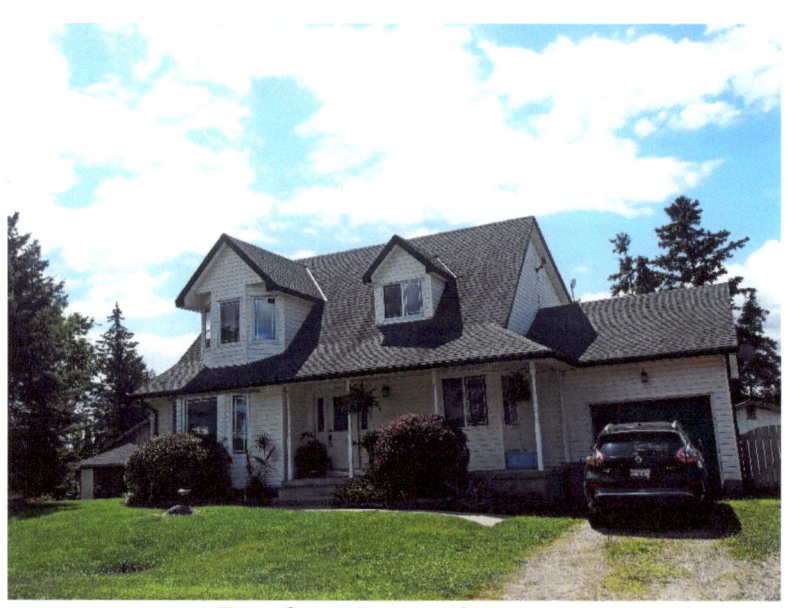

Dereham Line - dormers

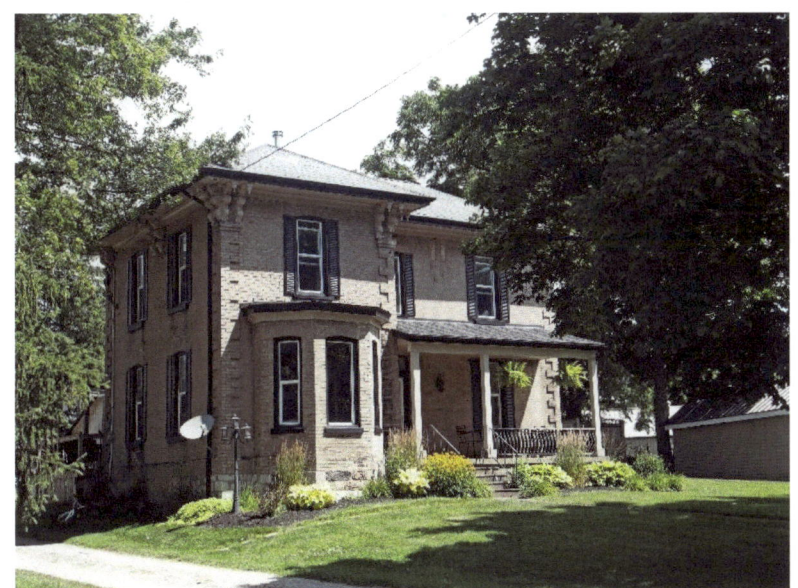

Dereham Line – Italianate – cornice brackets, corner quoins, bay window

Ostrander

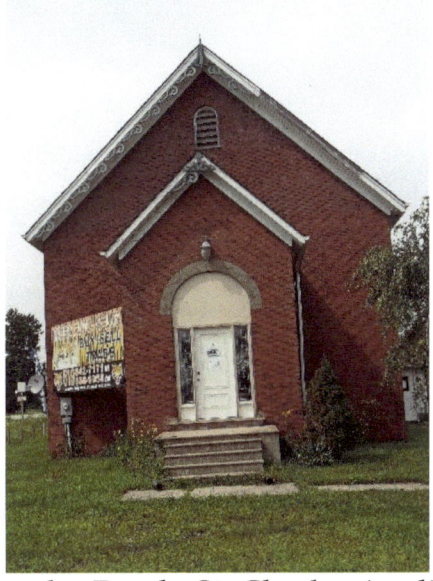

224570 Ostrander Road - St. Charles Anglican Church

Verschoyle

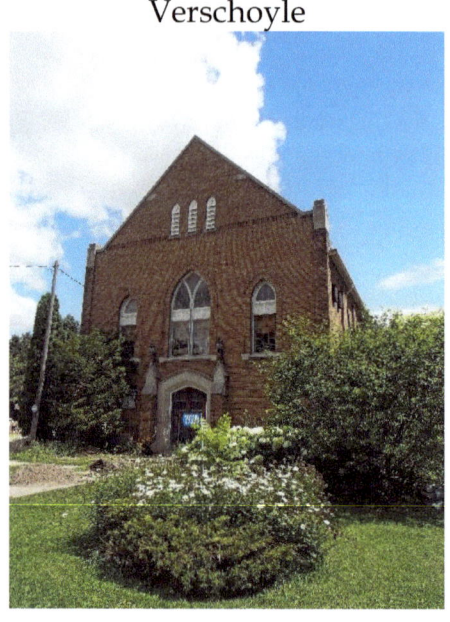

293218 Culloden Line - St Andrews United Church, Verschoyle - 1929

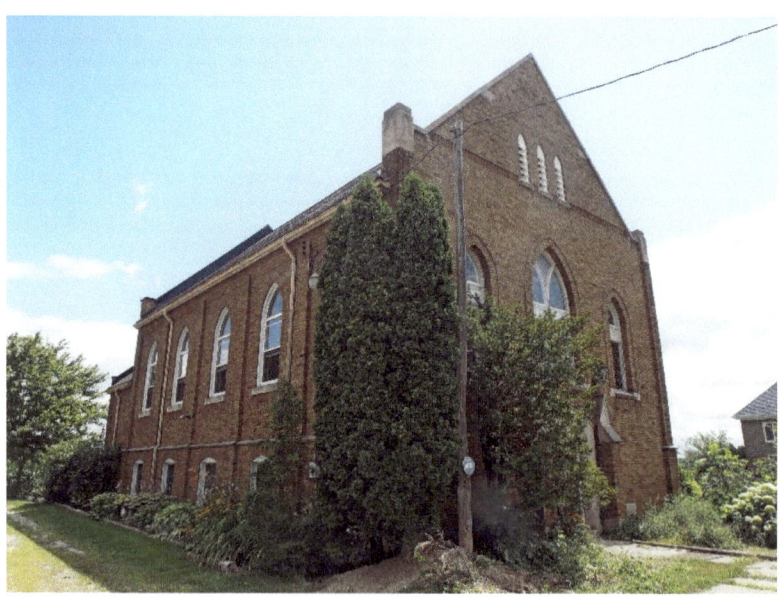

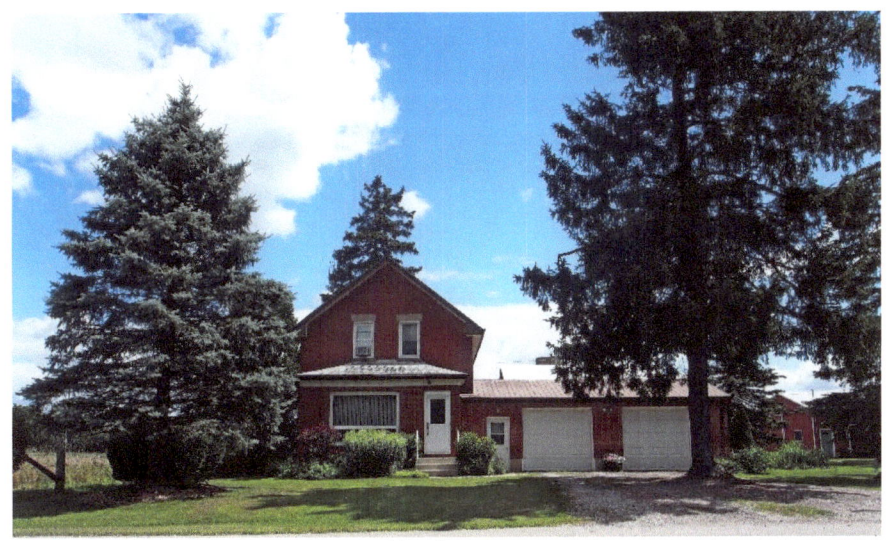

Culloden Line

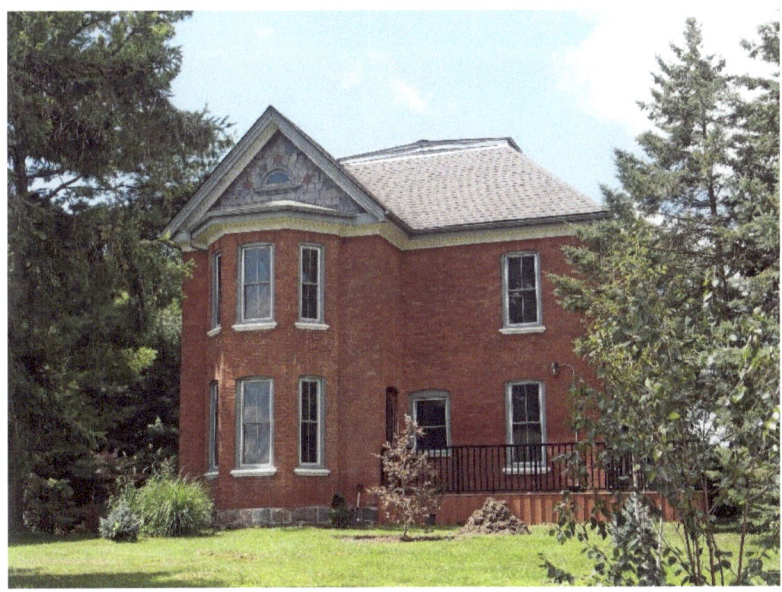

Culloden Line – two-storey bay window, fish scale patterning and semi-circular window in gable

Culloden

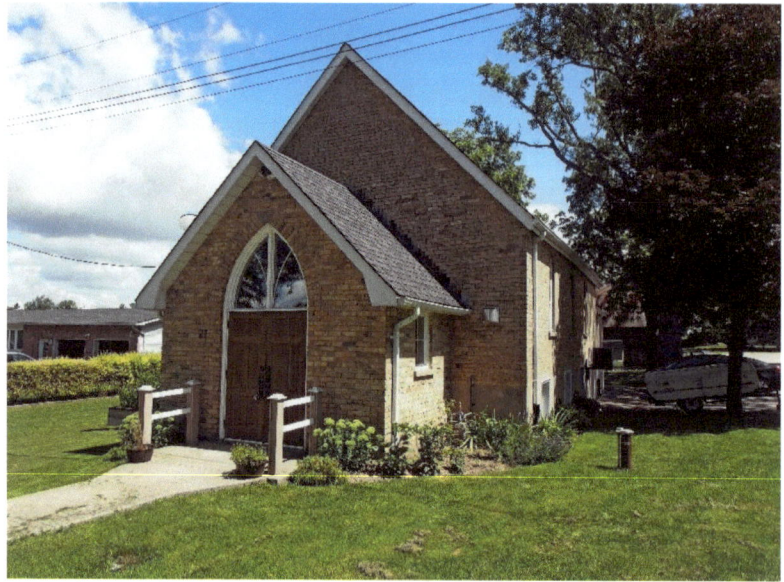

21 Richmond Street - Anglican Church - 1910

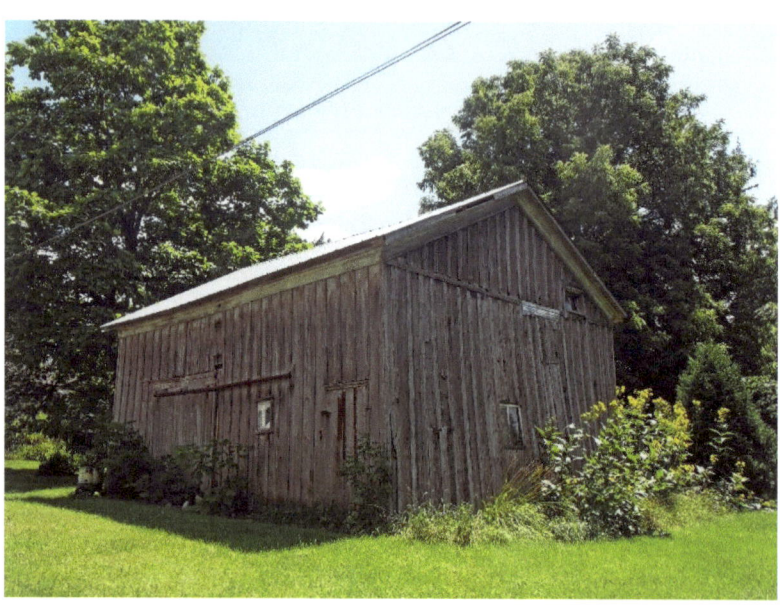

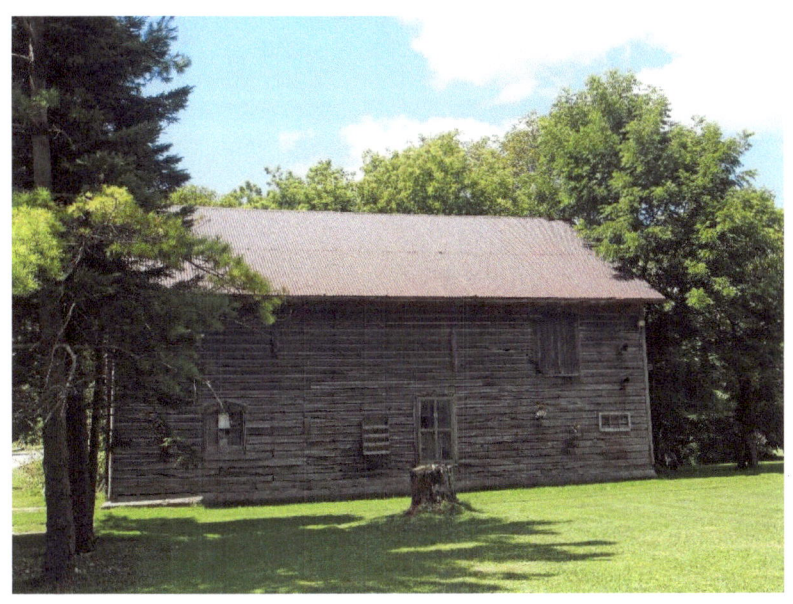

Brownsville

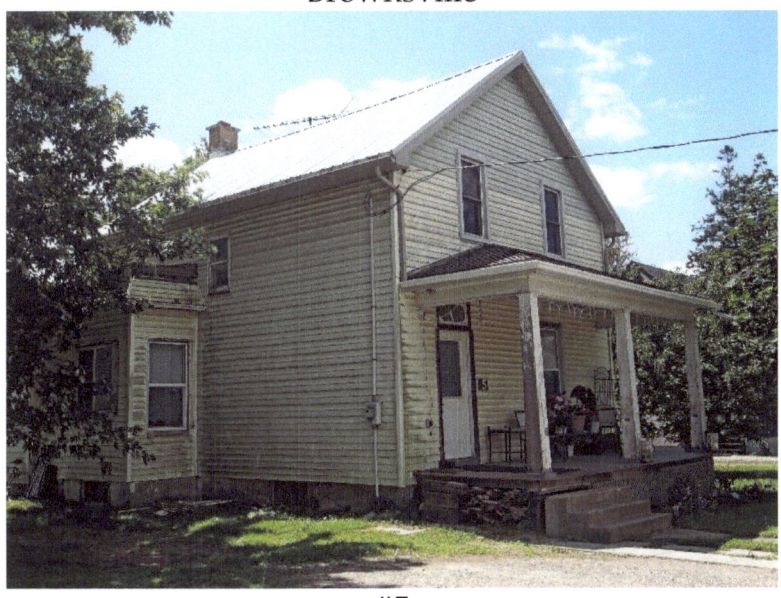

#5

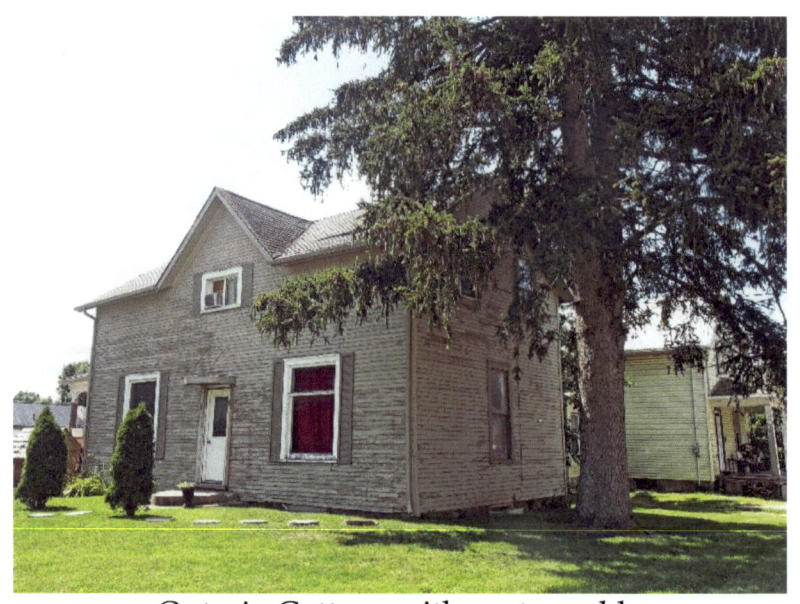

Ontario Cottage with center gable

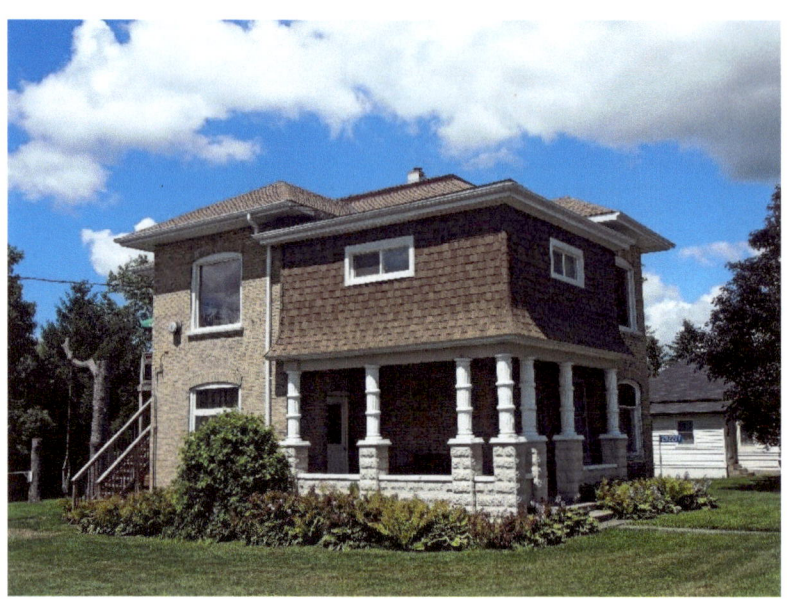

#292277

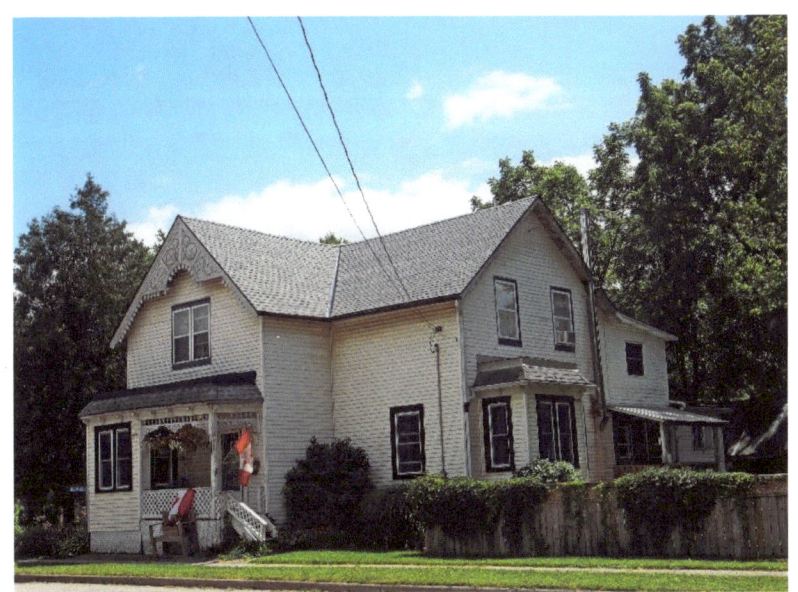
Gothic Revival – verge board trim on gable

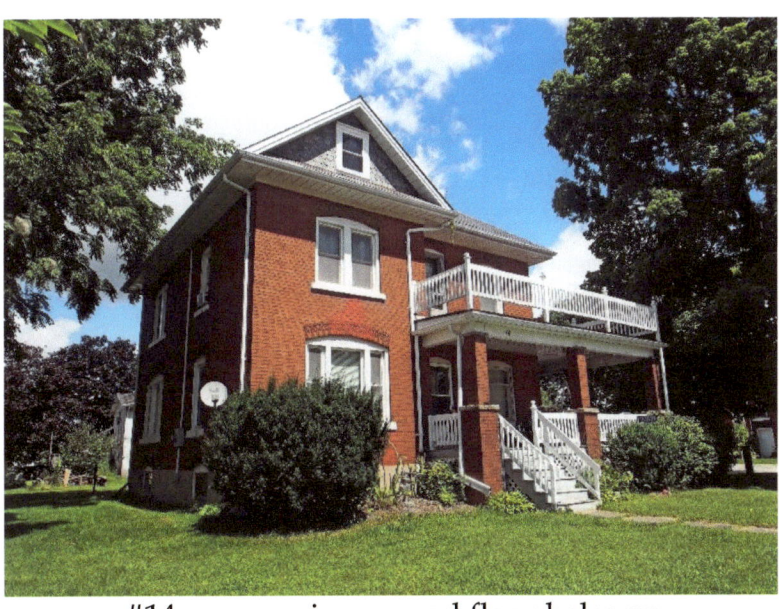
#14 – voussoirs, second floor balcony

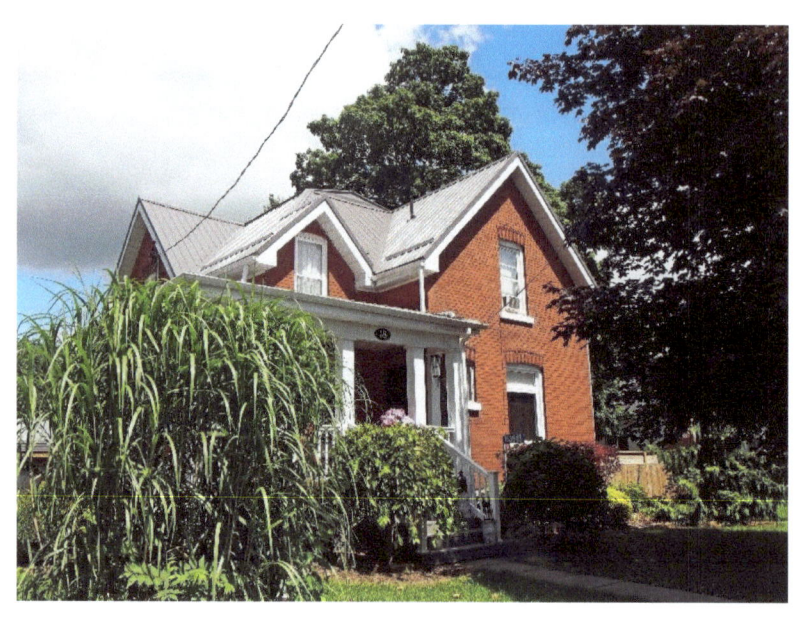

#18

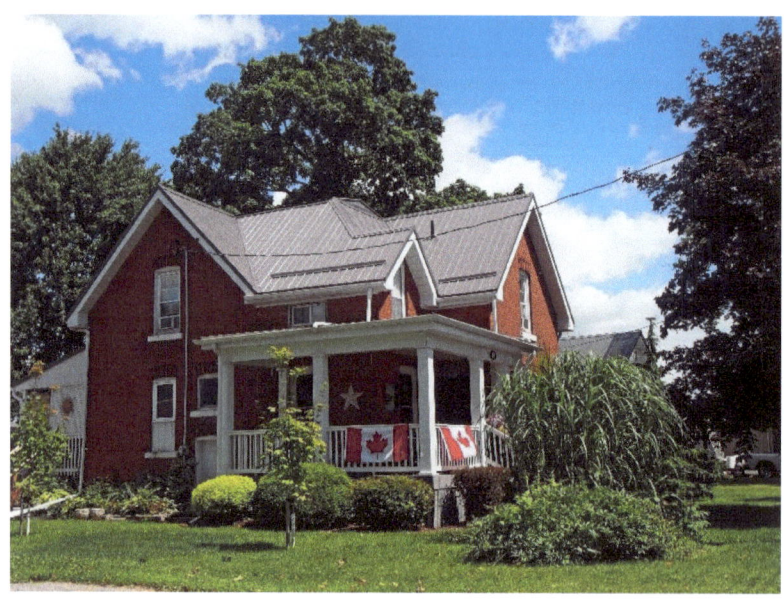

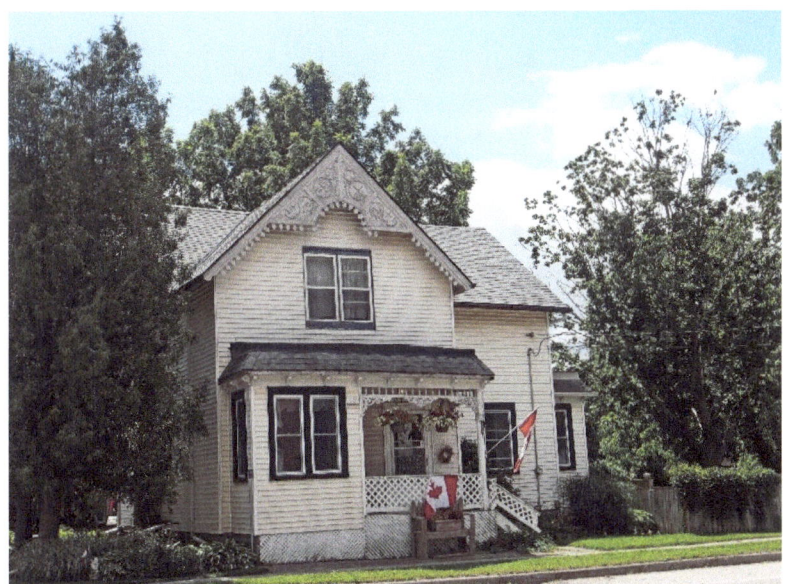

Verge board trim on gable

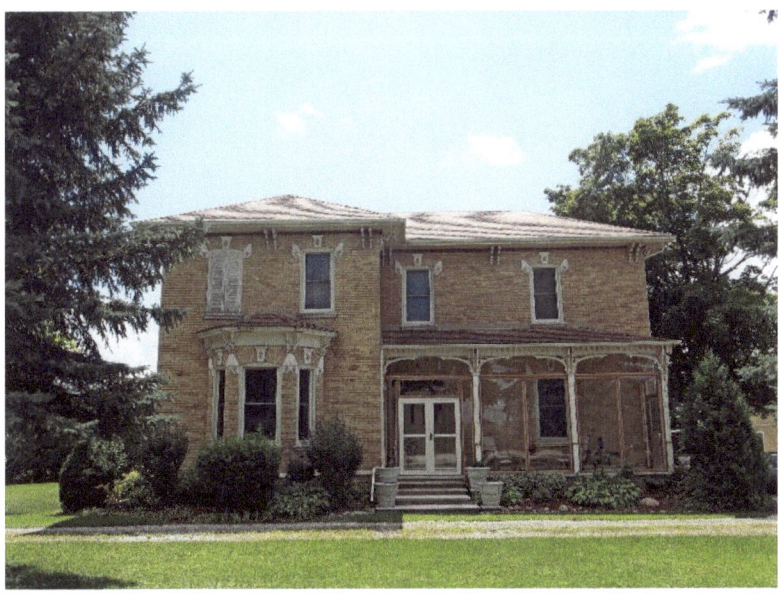

163576 – hipped roof, cornice brackets, dichromatic voussoirs, bay window with brackets, decorative porch

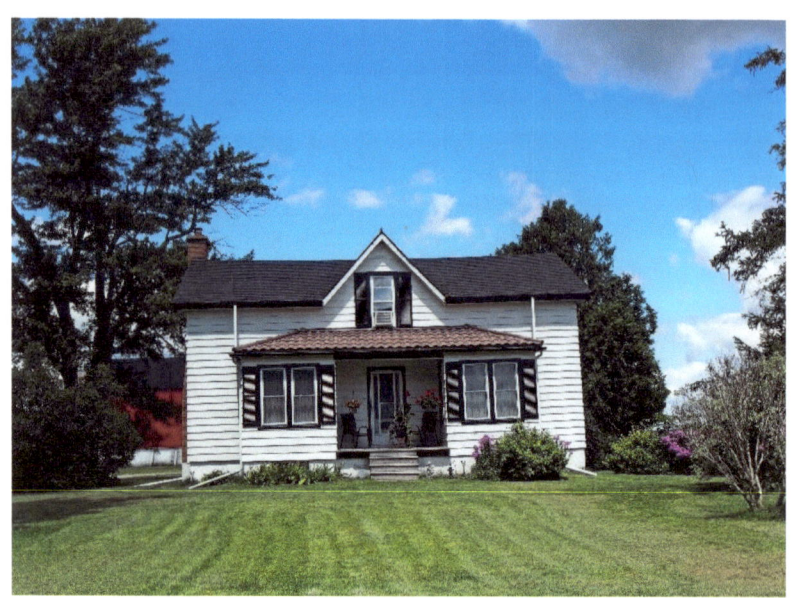
Regency Cottage with center gable

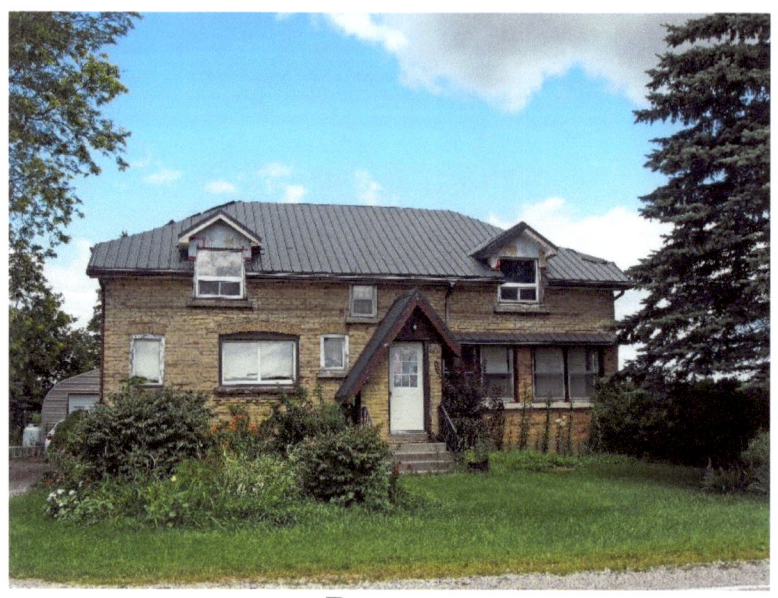
Dormers

Delmer

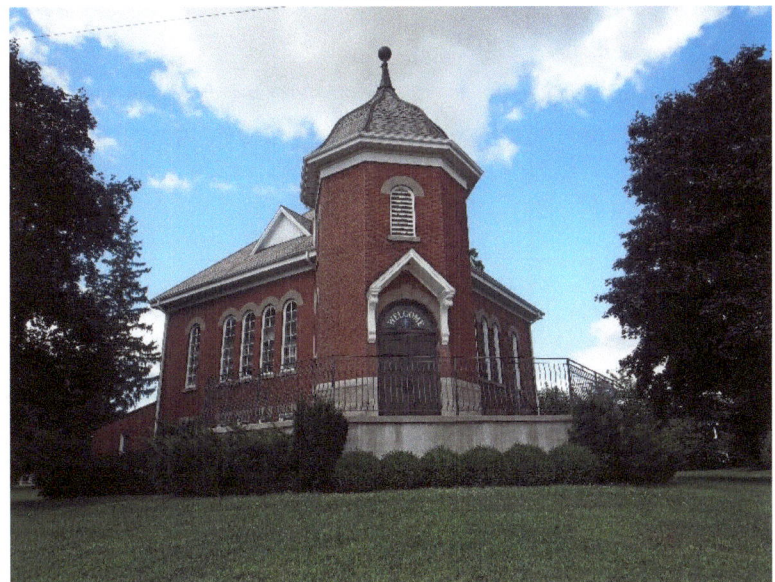

312281 Dereham Line - Delmer United Church – A.D. 1900

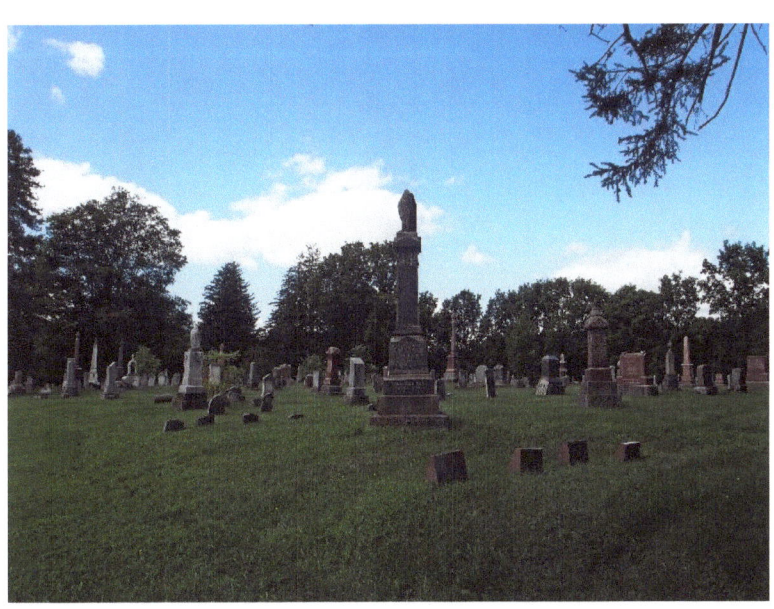

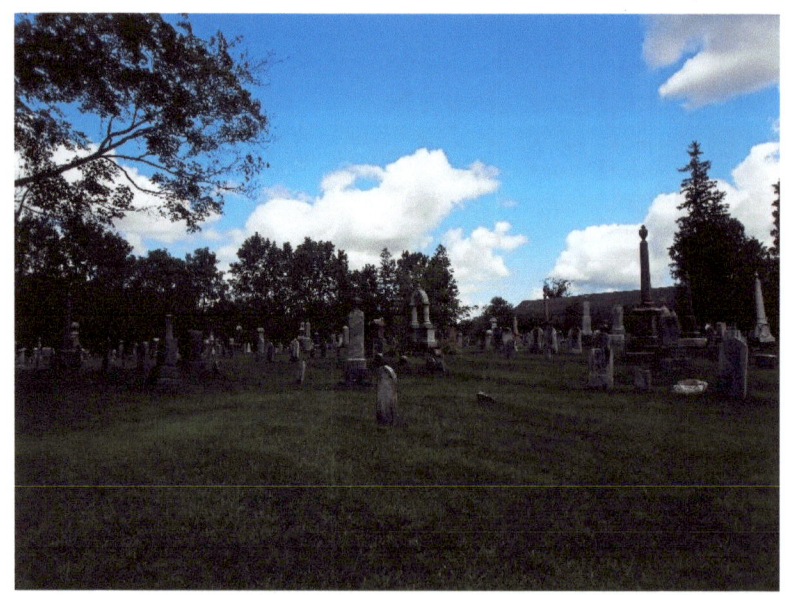
163891 Brownsville Road – Old Delmer Cemetery

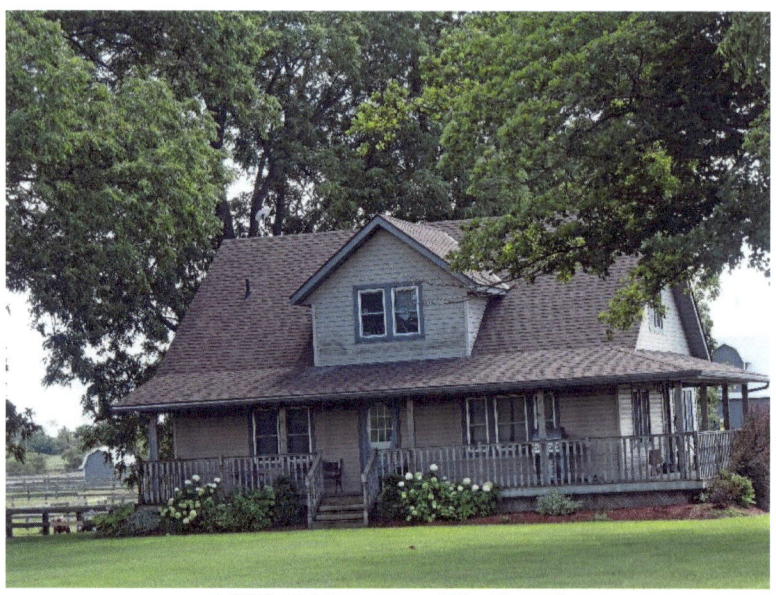
163942 Brownsville Road

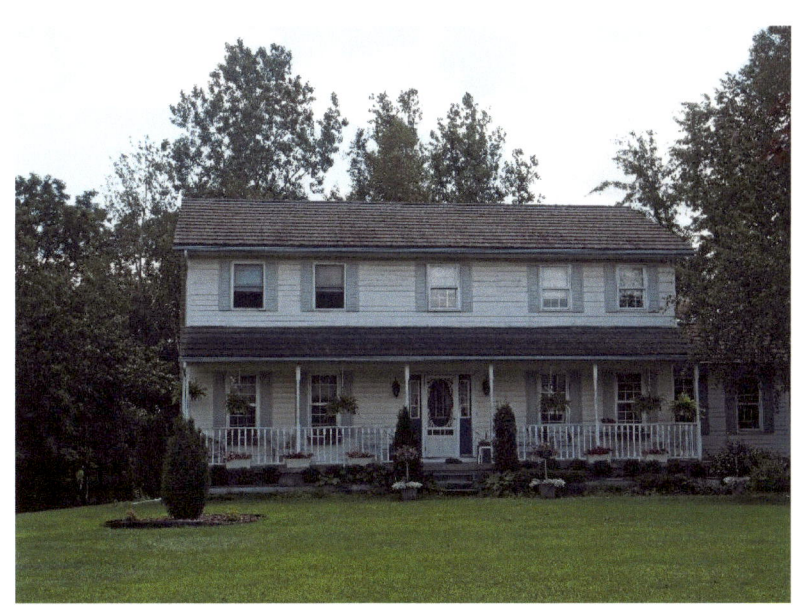

Brownsville Road

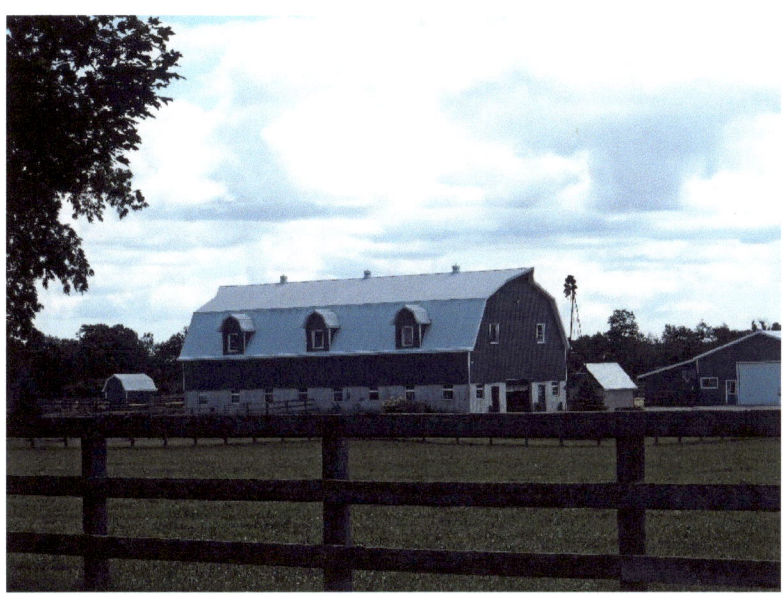

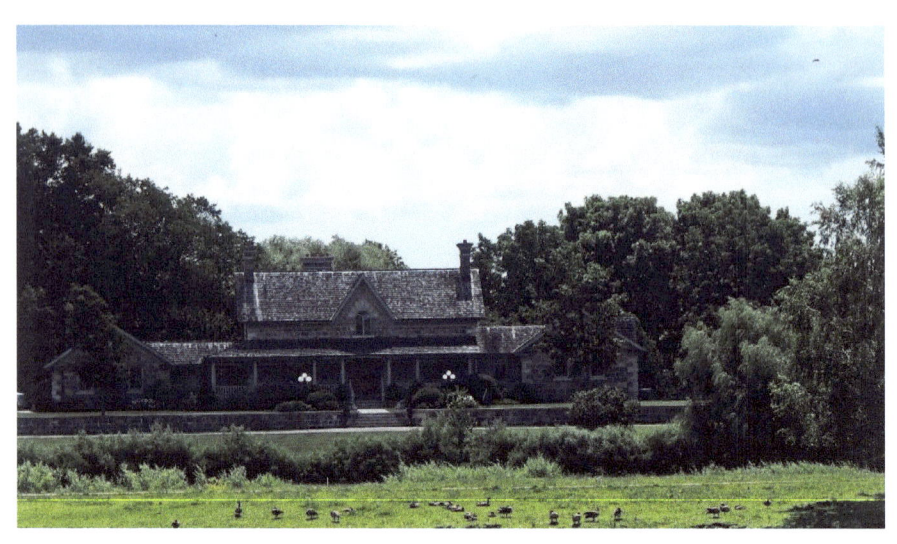

McLaughlin Family Farm

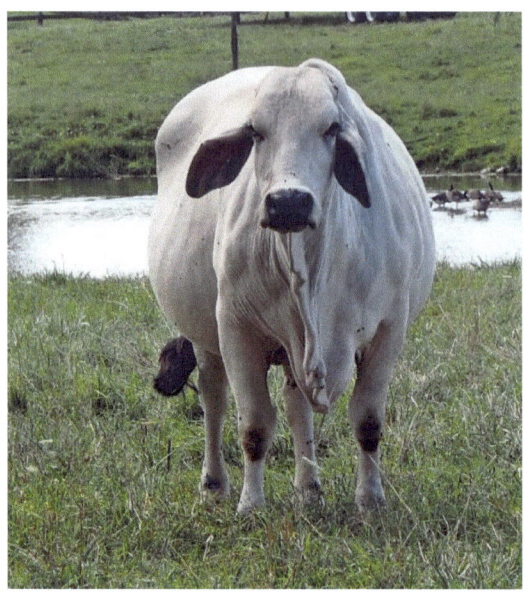

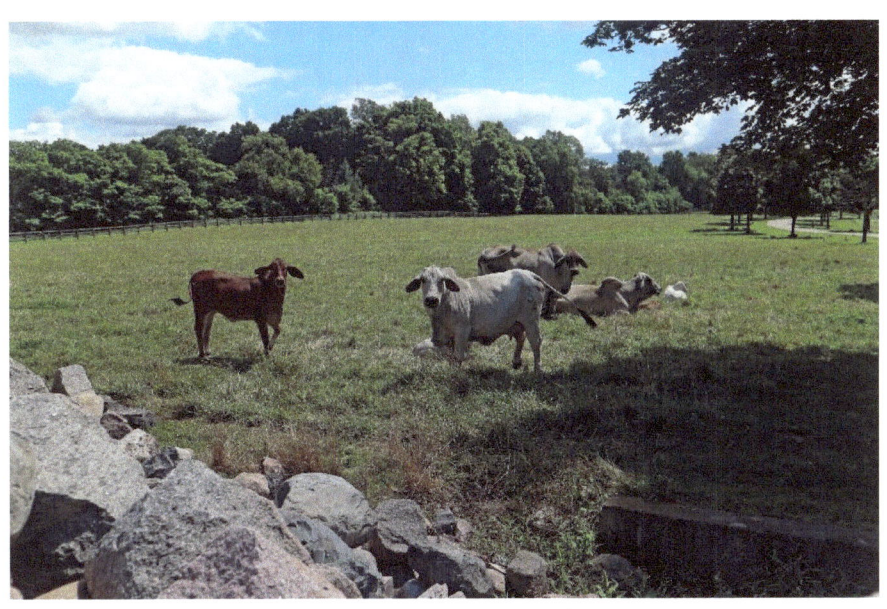

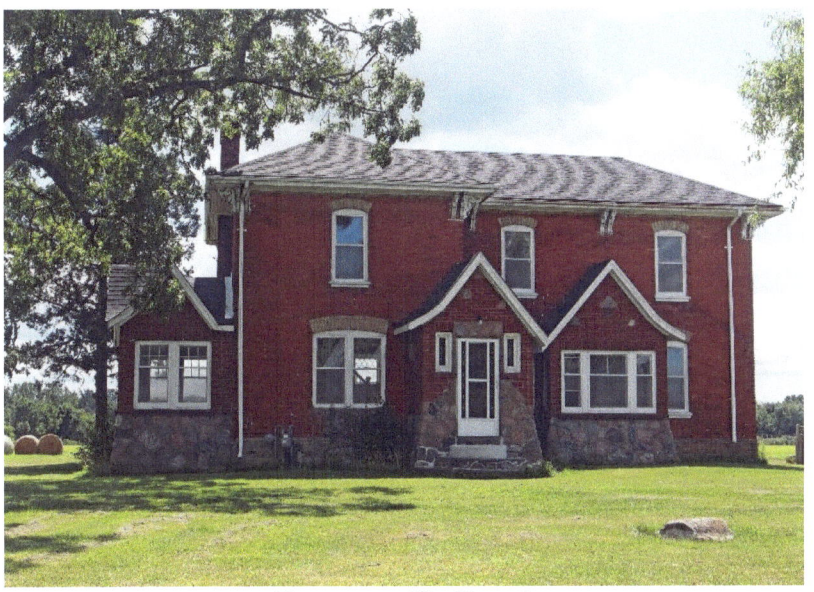

Brownsville Road

Beachville

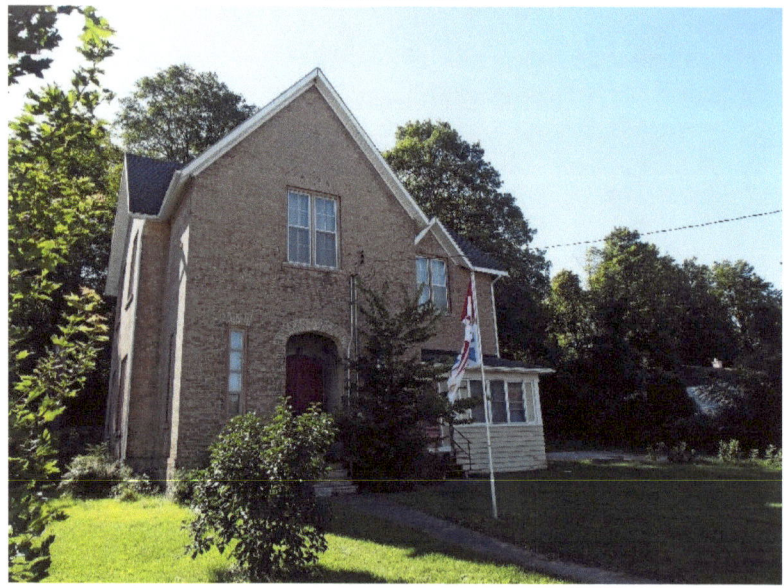

584572 Beachville Road – former Beachville Anglican Church

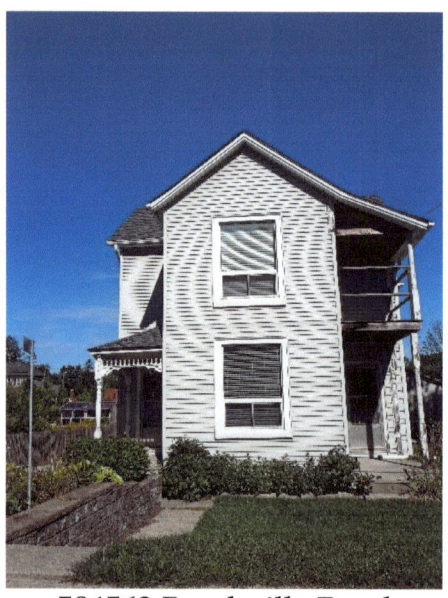

584563 Beachville Road

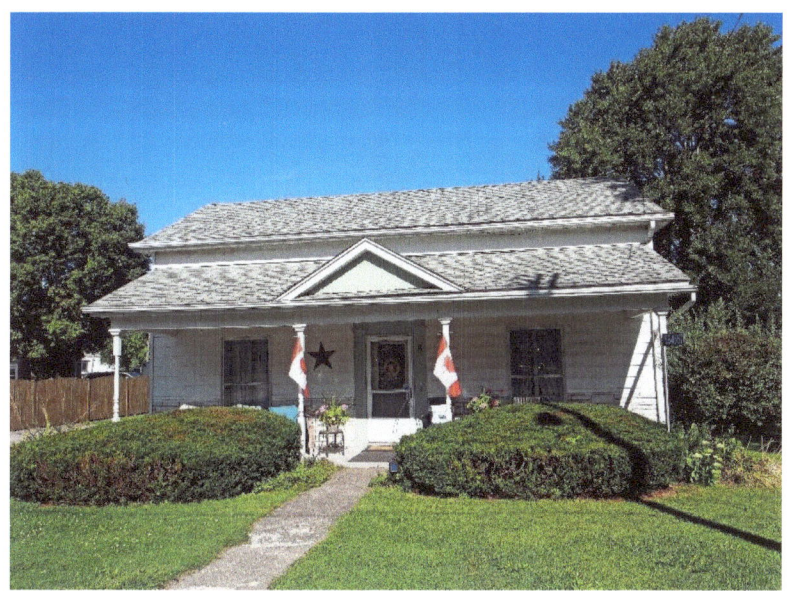

584557 Beachville Road

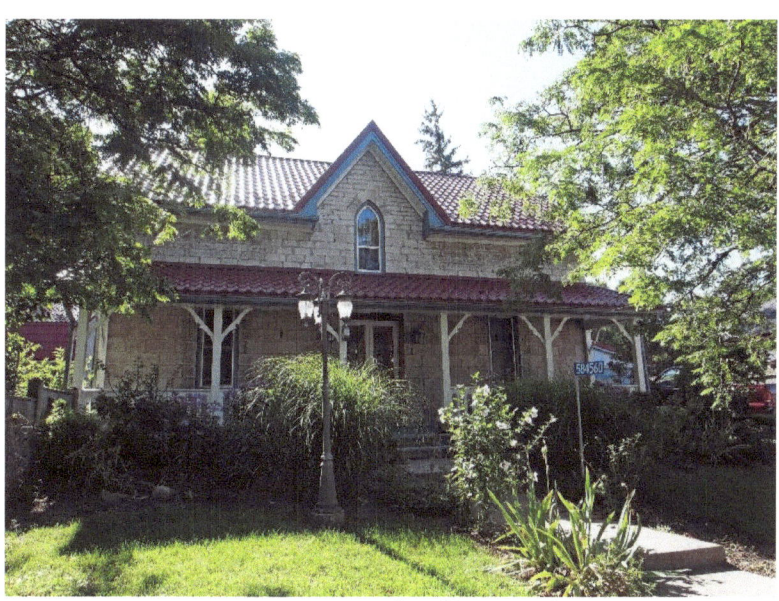

584560 Beachville Road

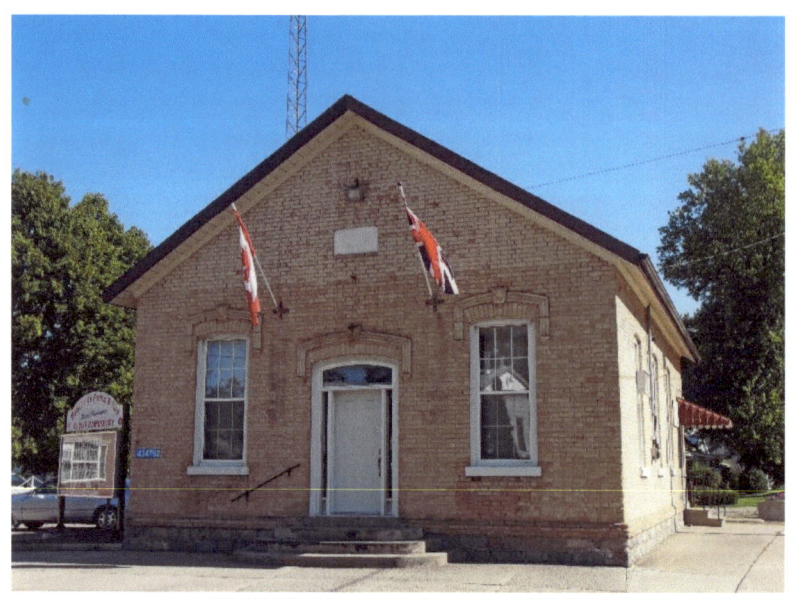

434792 Zorra Line – c. 1867

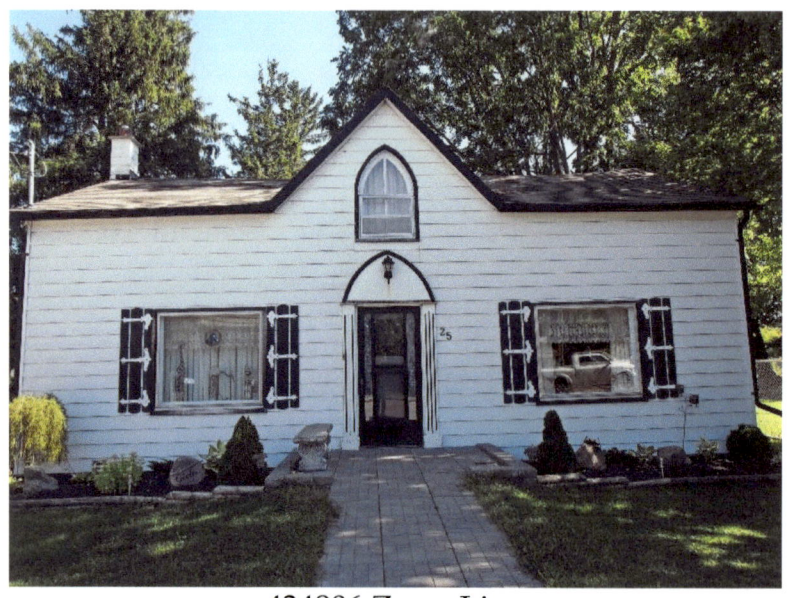

434806 Zorra Line

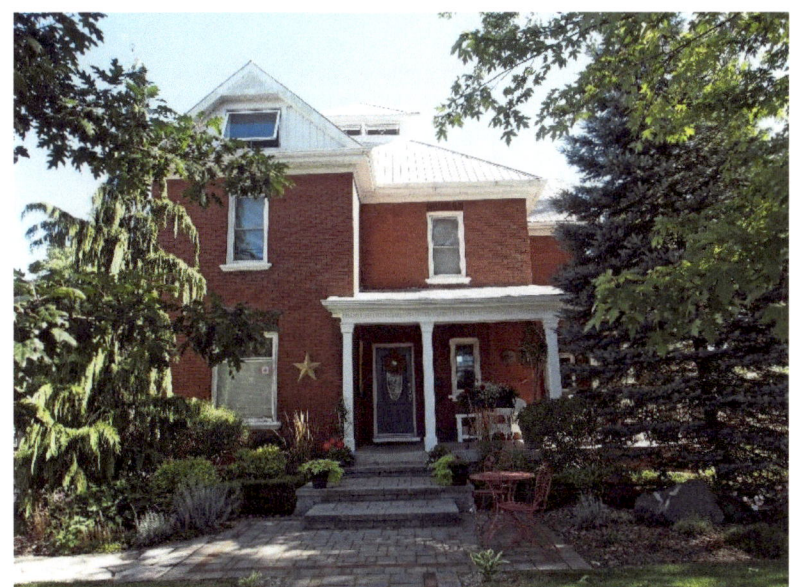

434808 Zorra Line

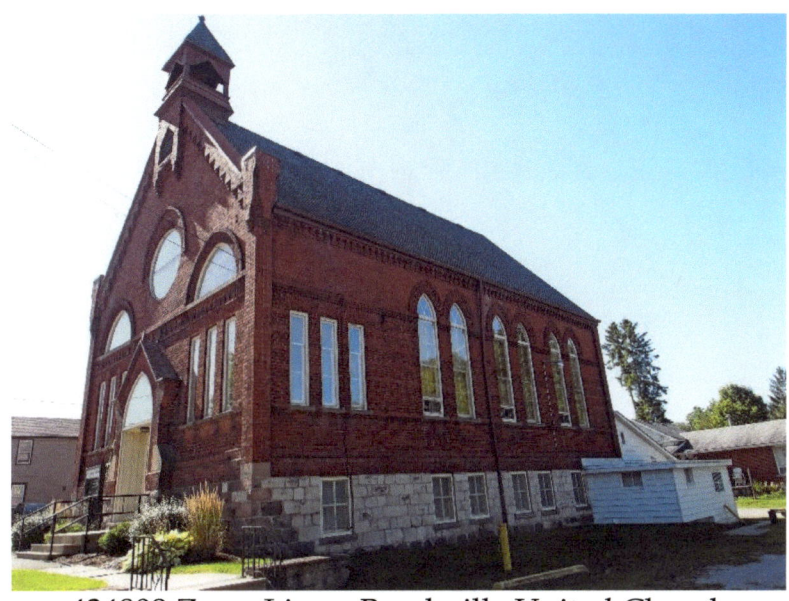

434809 Zorra Line – Beachville United Church

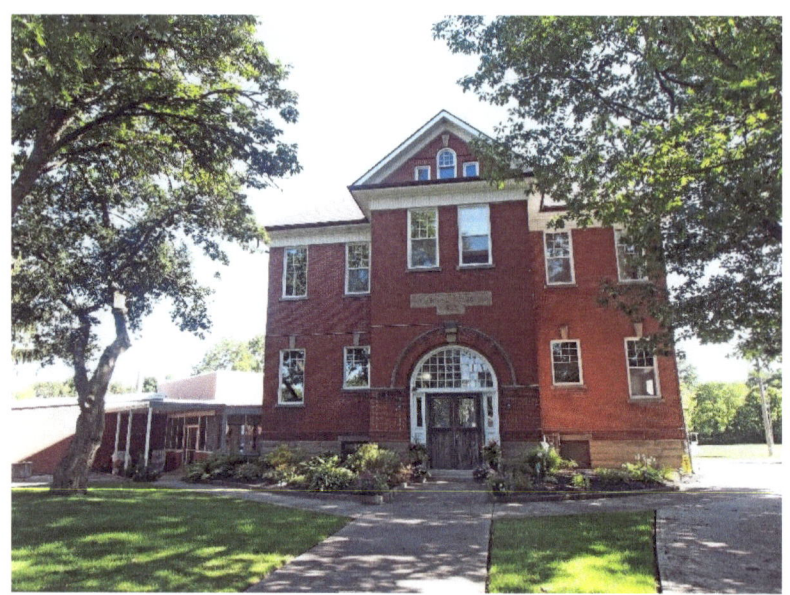

434804 Zorra Line - Central Public School

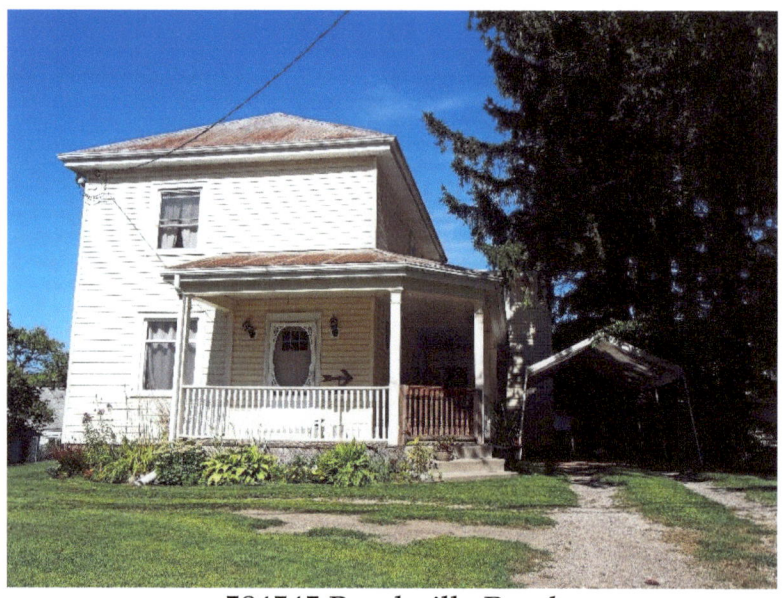

584545 Beachville Road

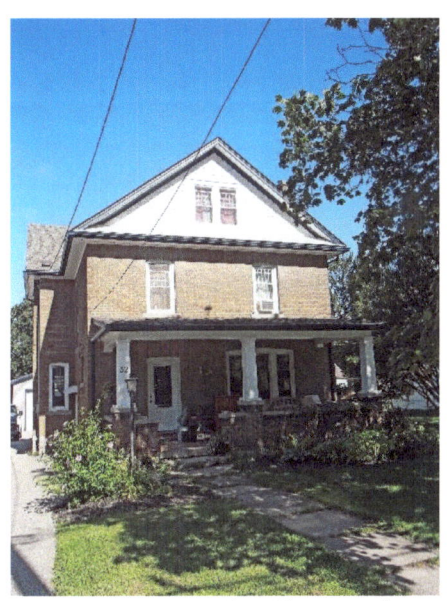

584513 Beachville Road

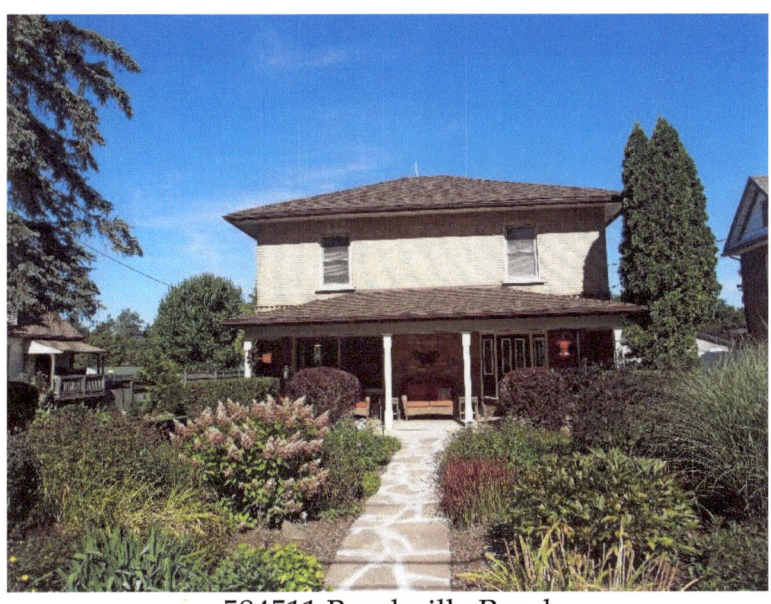

584511 Beachville Road

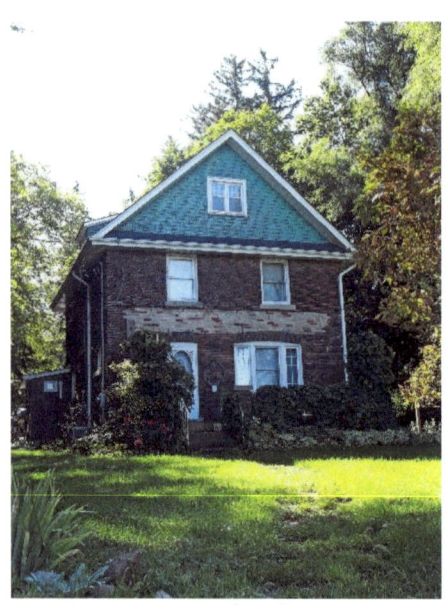

584510 Beachville Road

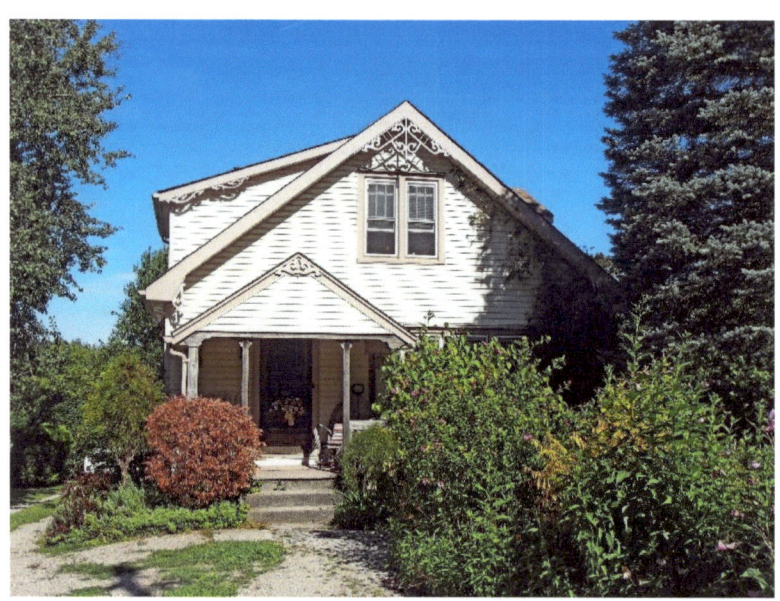

584509 Beachville Road

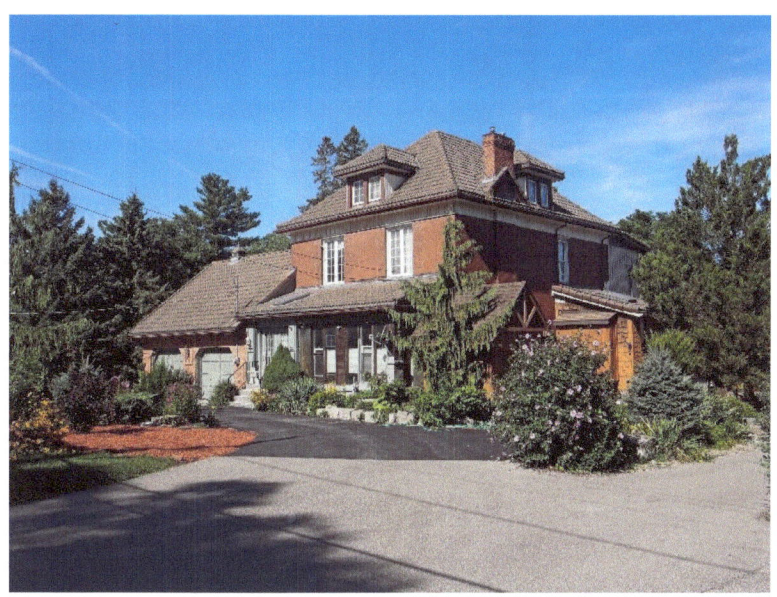

584503 Beachville Road

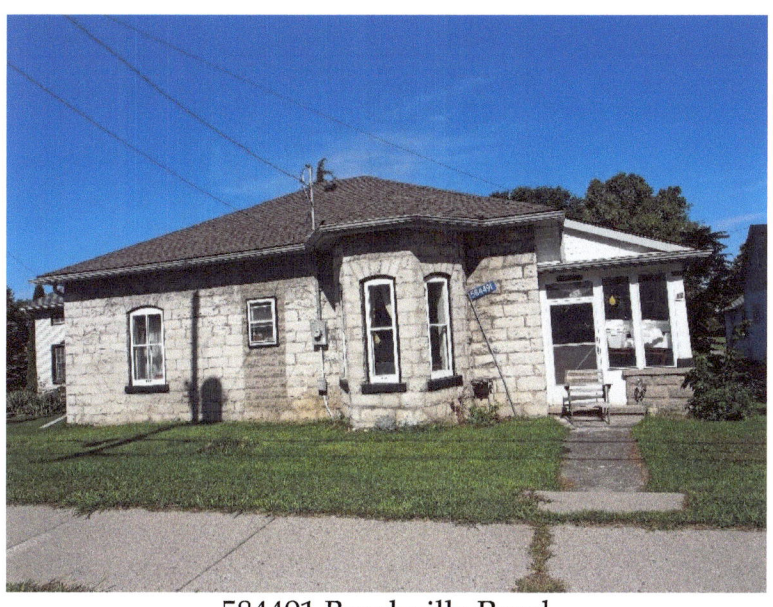

584491 Beachville Road

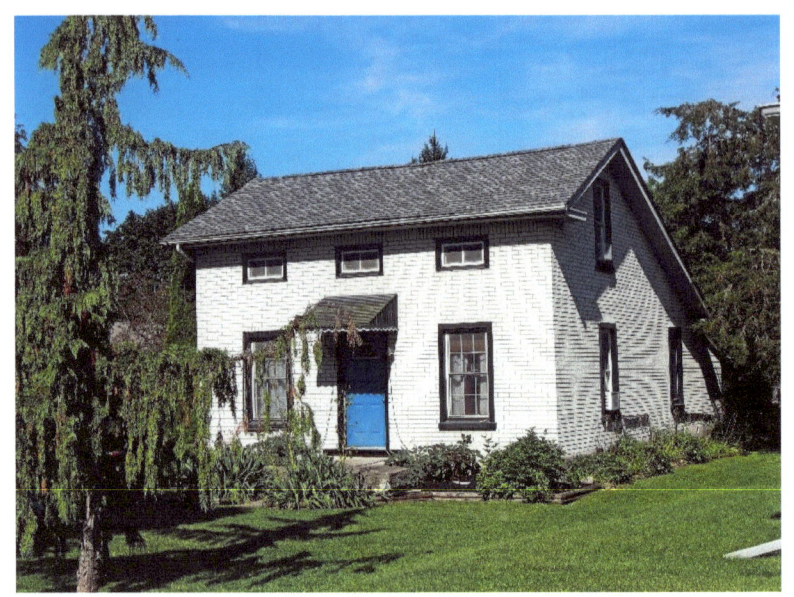

Beachville Road

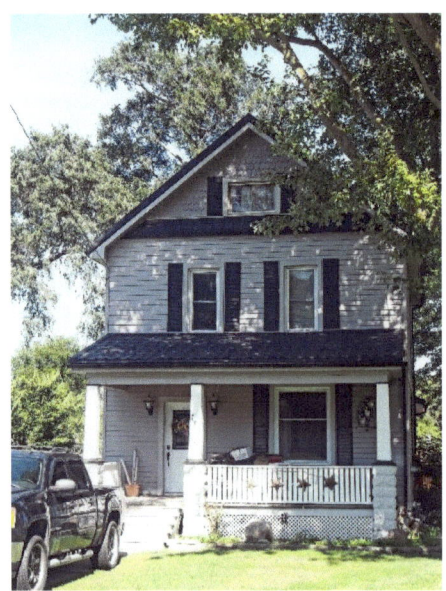

584467 Beachville Road

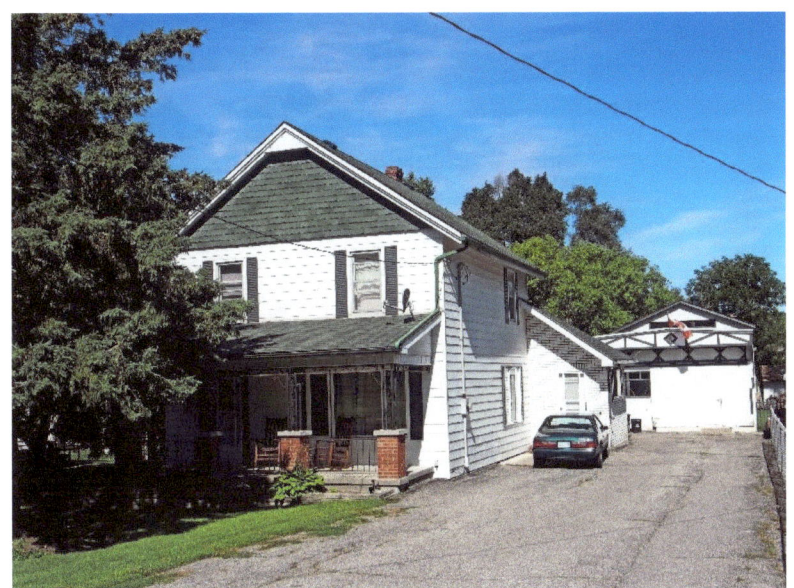

584463 Beachville Road

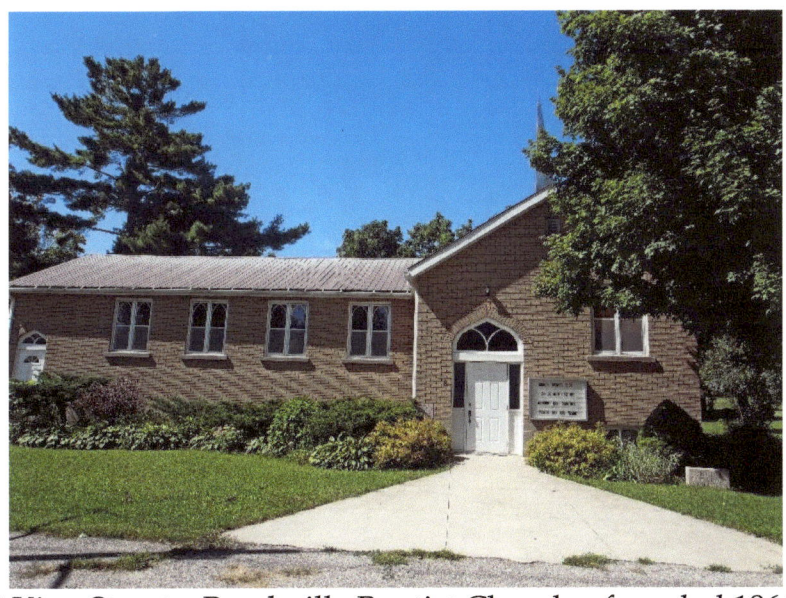

8 King Street – Beachville Baptist Church – founded 1866, burned 1943, rebuilt 1948

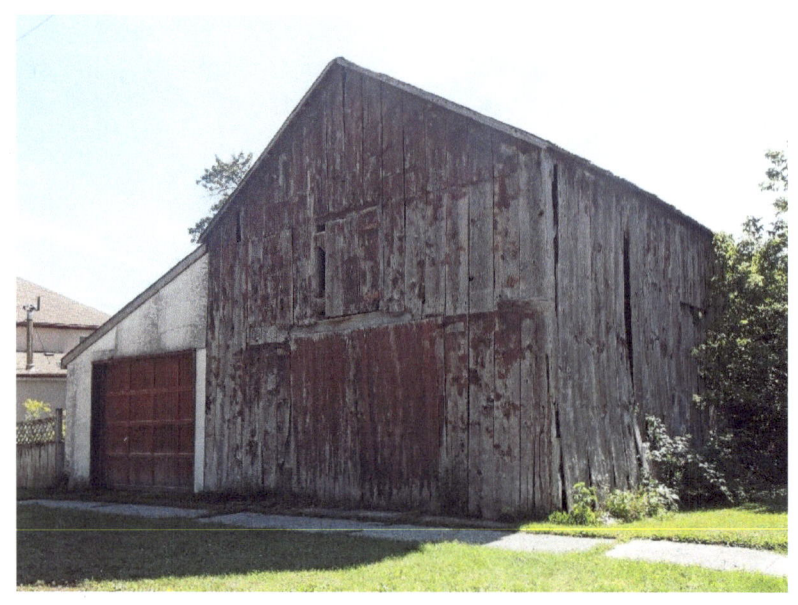

Beachville District Museum

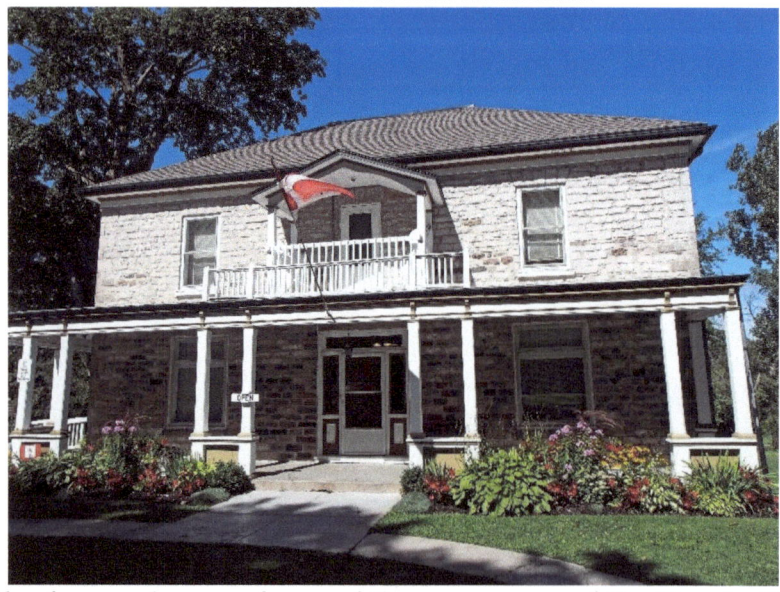

The former home of one of the managers of the Beachville quarry – The Downings

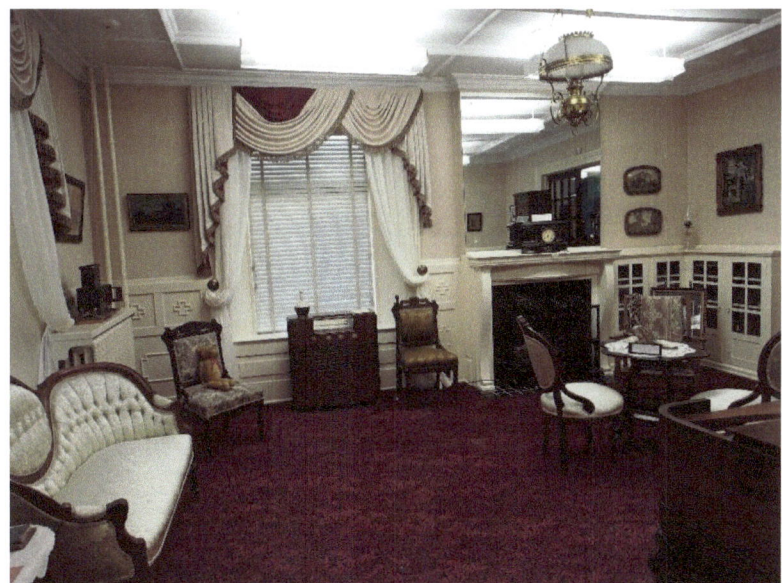

The salon, or living room, was the focal point of the Downings' social life in the nineteenth and twentieth centuries. They kept themselves entertained with pianos, violins and radios.

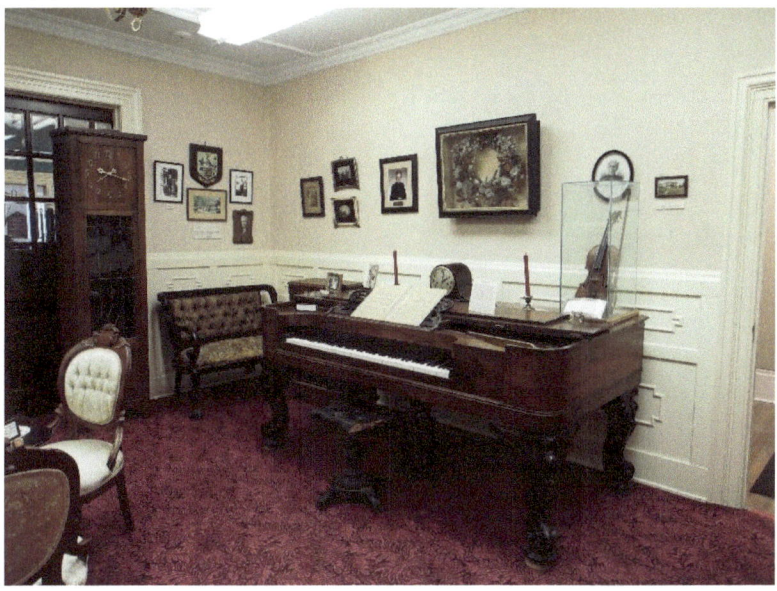

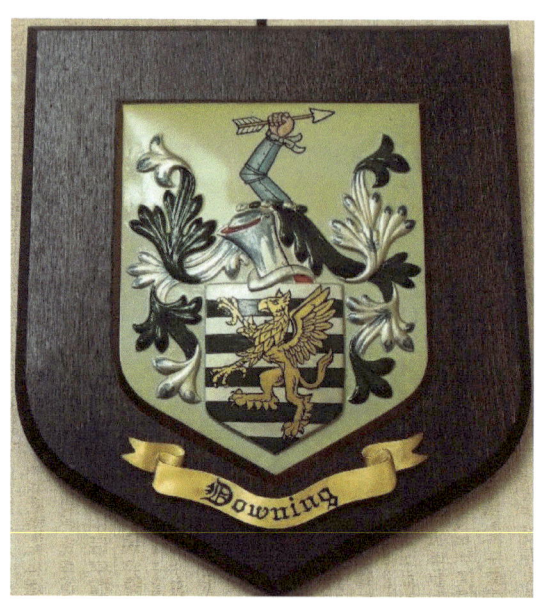

Downing Crest

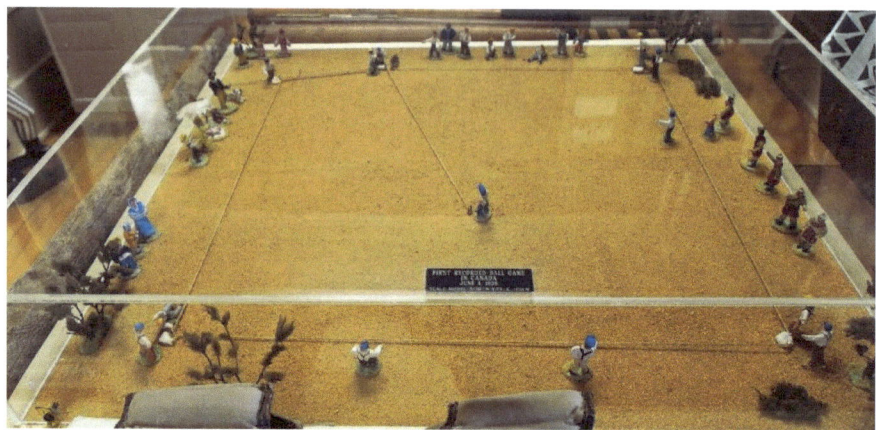

The first recorded baseball game in North America was played in Beachville on June 4, 1838. The competing teams were from Beachville and the combined townships of Zorra and North Oxford. The ball used was made of double and twisted wool yarn covered with calf skin and sewn with waxed ends. The club (bat) was a straight stick of cedar such as a wagon spoke.

Beachville's Limestone Quarries

Limestone is a sedimentary rock. The Egyptians made the pyramids out of limestone. In the early days, limestone rocks were picked out of the river until there was hardly any remaining. Then limestone was mined in quarries in the ground. The rocks were crushed to reduce their size before they went to the kiln. A kiln is a big oven which heats up the rock. When the limestone rock is under high temperatures, it goes through a metamorphosis. When the rock is cool, it is lime and can then be used in many different ways.

Pioneers discovered that limestone could be baked and then used as plaster to fill gaps between logs in their cabin walls. Whitewash (paint) can also be made from lime. Ground limestone can be used as cement, or fashioned to make homes and other buildings. The second floor of the Beachville District Museum is built with limestone.

Present day uses of limestone: absorbs impurities in steel manufacture, keeps acid at the right level in sewage treatment, removes Sulphur pollution in smoke stacks, improves drinking water quality, treats lakes that have been affected by acid rain. It can be ground and used to make cement or bricks, or it can be mixed with sand and soda ash to make glass. It reduces acid in cream to make butter, absorbs moisture in rubber manufacturing, acts as a base for chemical fertilizer, is used in production of sugar, varnish and paper, and ground limestone mixed with chicken feed eases the animal's digestion.

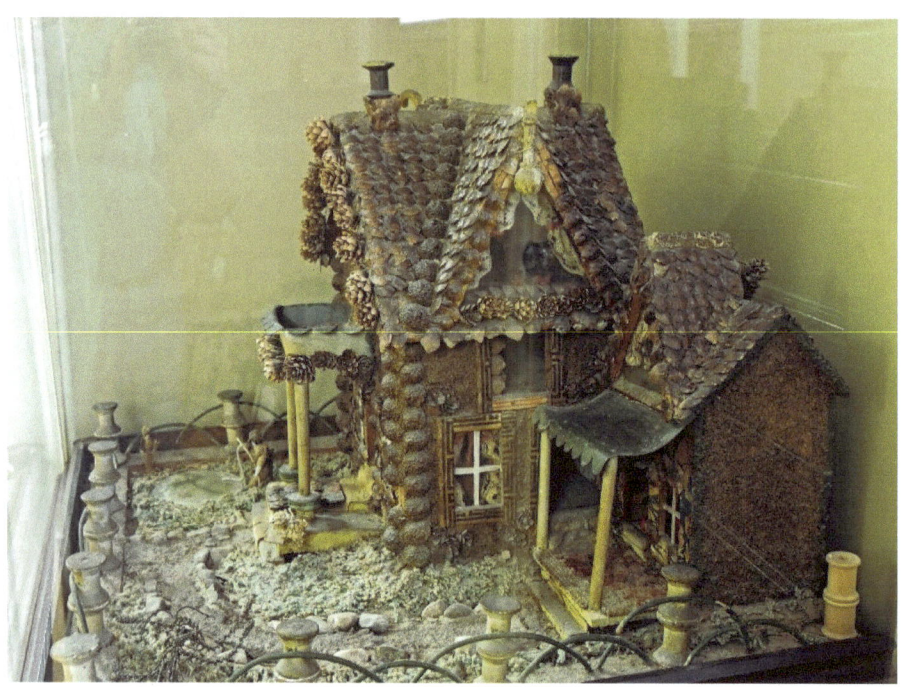

1855 Doll House: This handmade doll house belonged to Mrs. Sophia Hiram of Mount Elgin. The exterior is decorated with pine cones and acorns, and the fence is made with spools. There is a walkway made of pebbles, and green fabric is used for grass. Inside the house, china dolls pose with miniature furniture.

Norwich Township – Oxford Centre

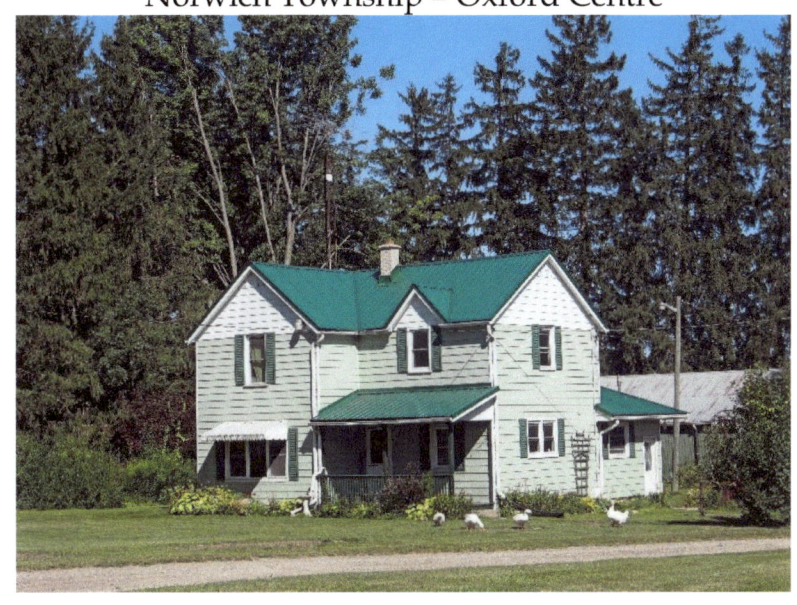

#525715

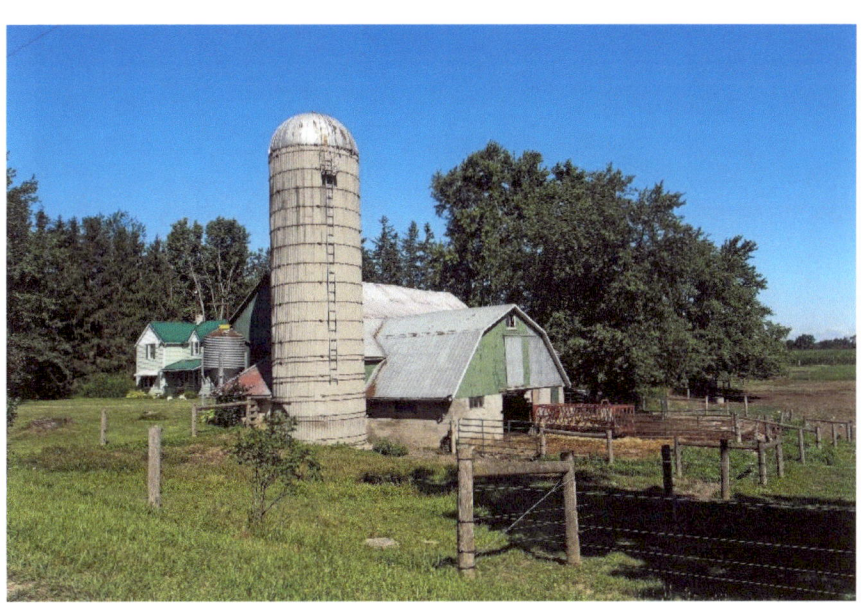

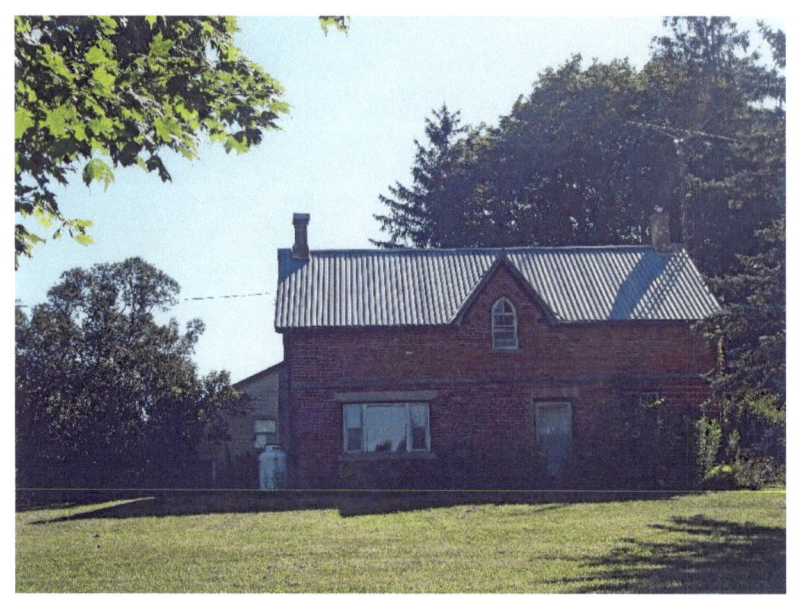

#774798 - Century Farm

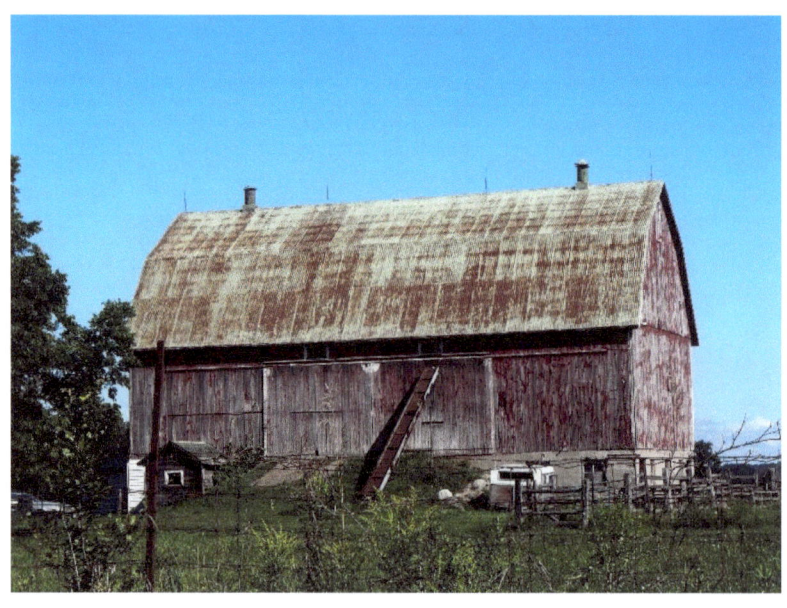

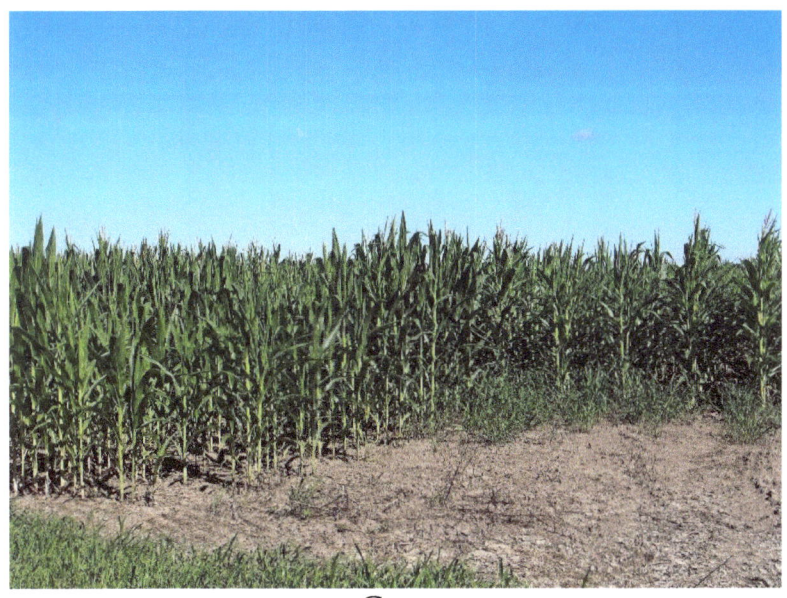

Corn

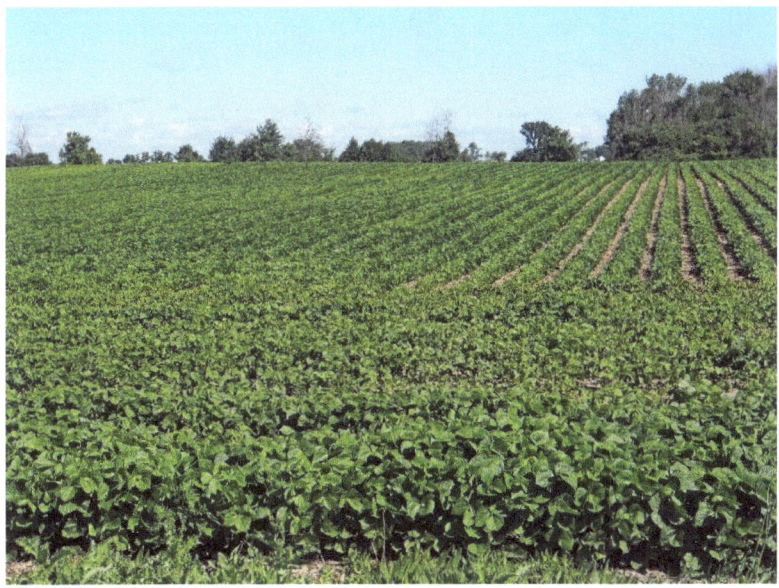

Soybeans

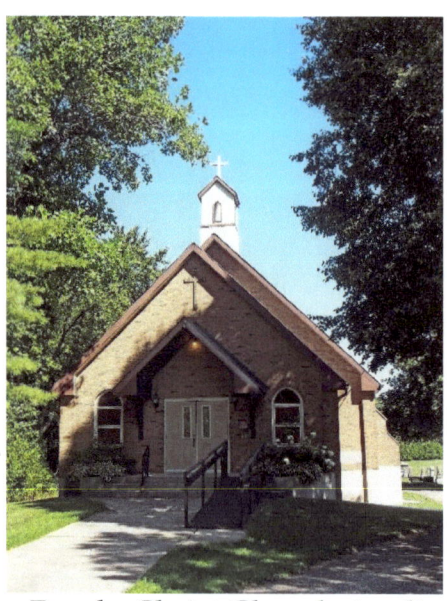

505395 Old Stage Road - Christ Church Anglican – built 1980 to replace original building destroyed by a tornado

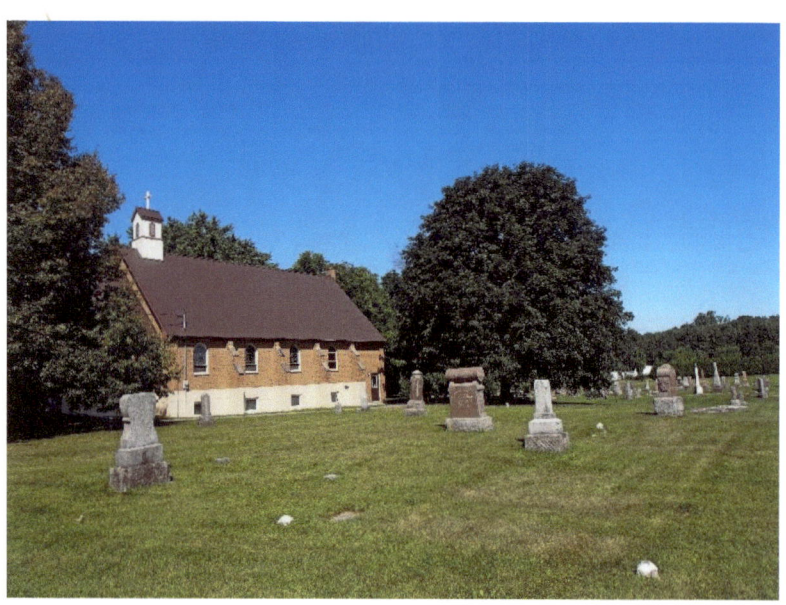

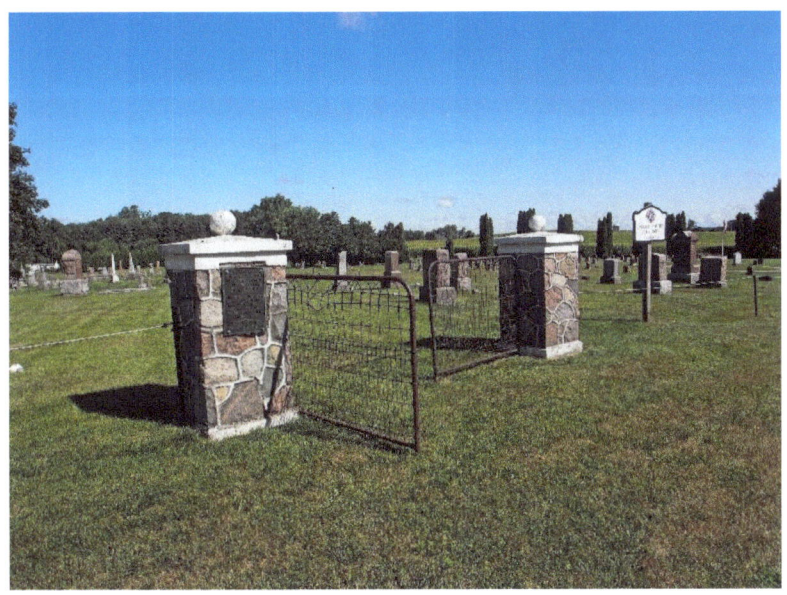

Anglican Cemetery – burial ground of United Empire Loyalists

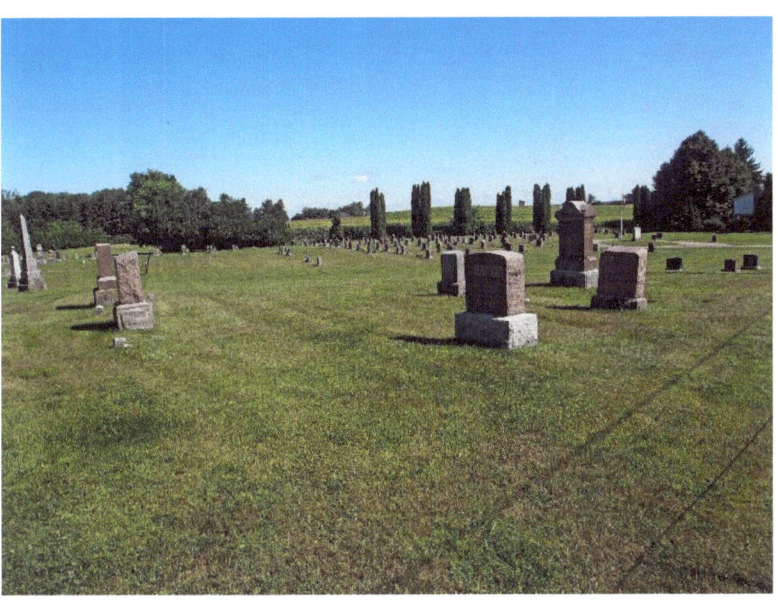

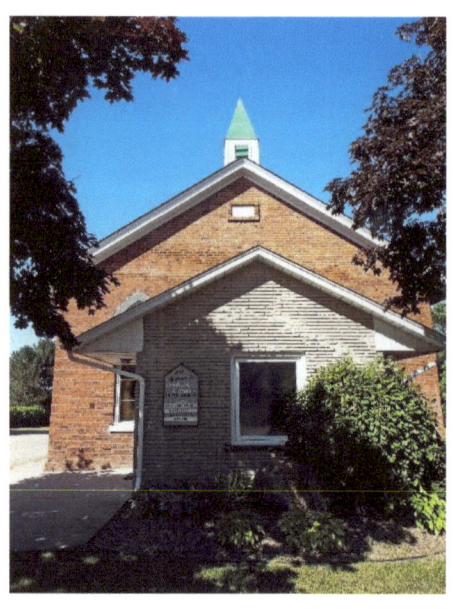

714581 Middletown Line - United Church – (Wesleyan) 1860

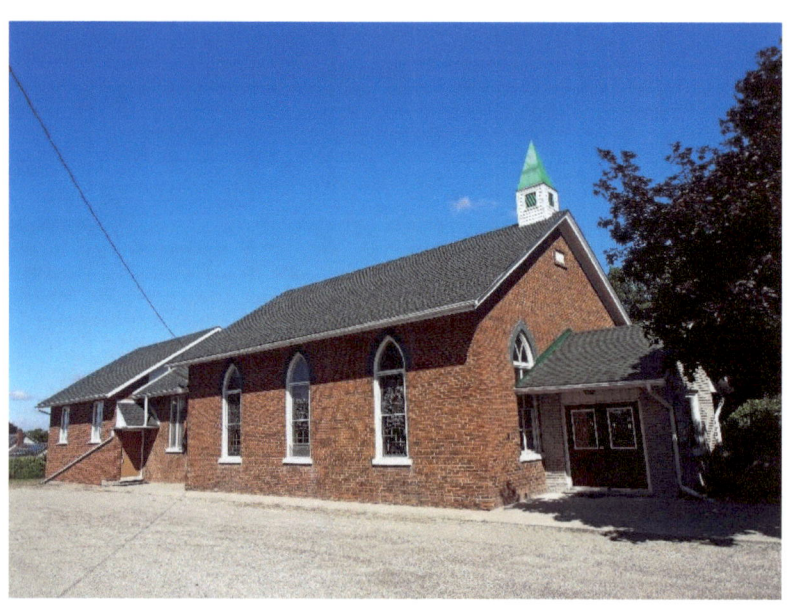

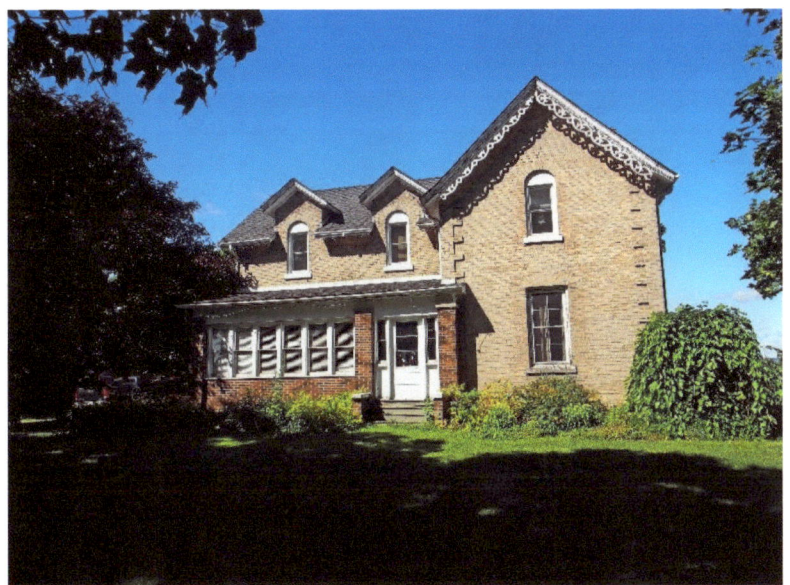

Gothic – verge board trim on gable, corner quoins, dormers

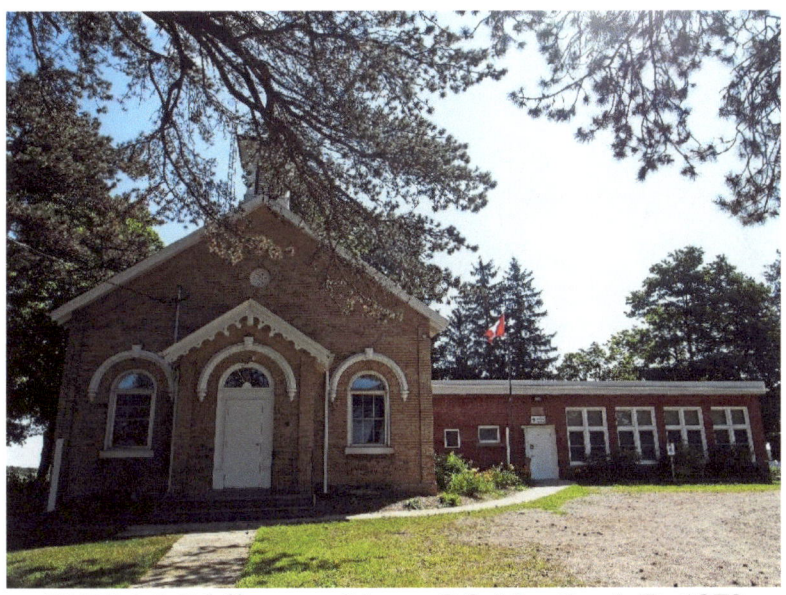

714516 Middletown Line – S.S. No. 5 – A.D. 1872

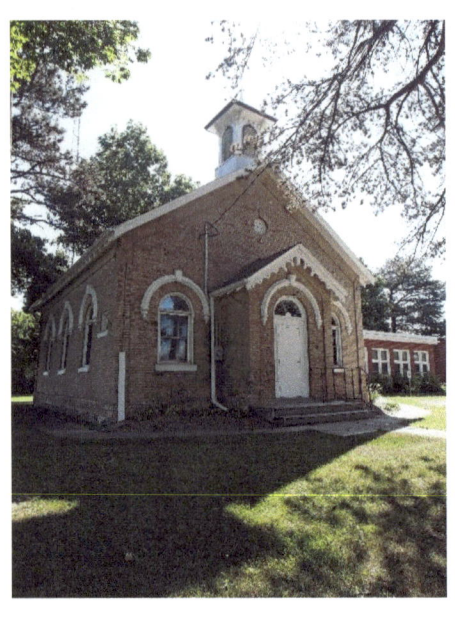

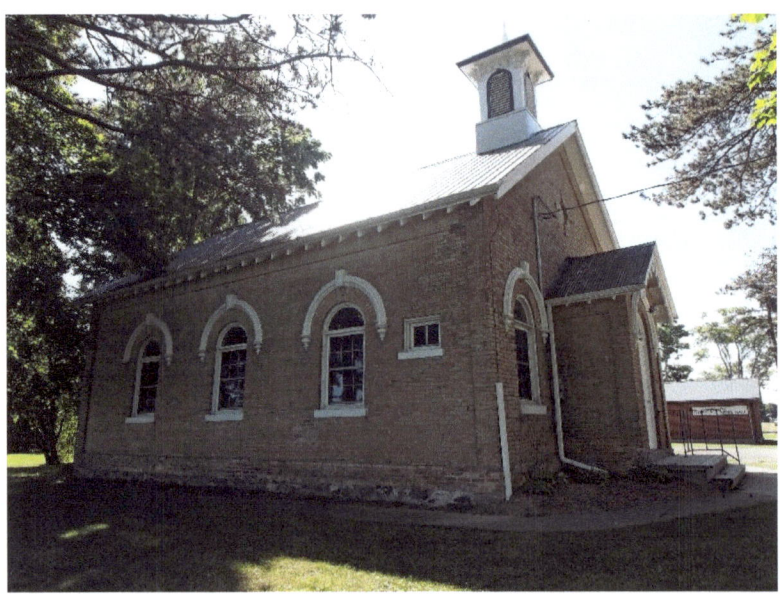

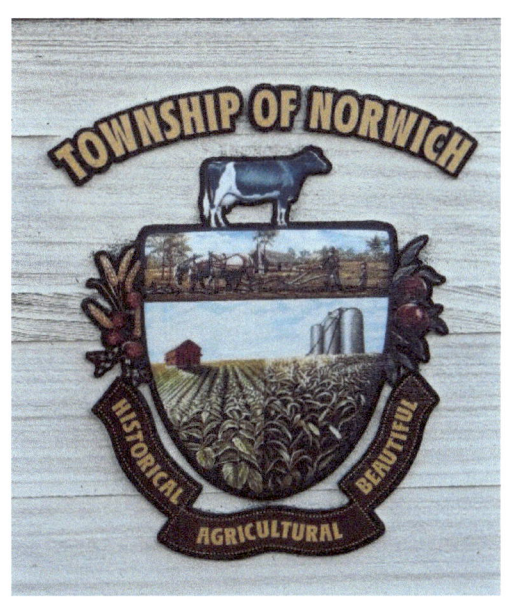

Curries

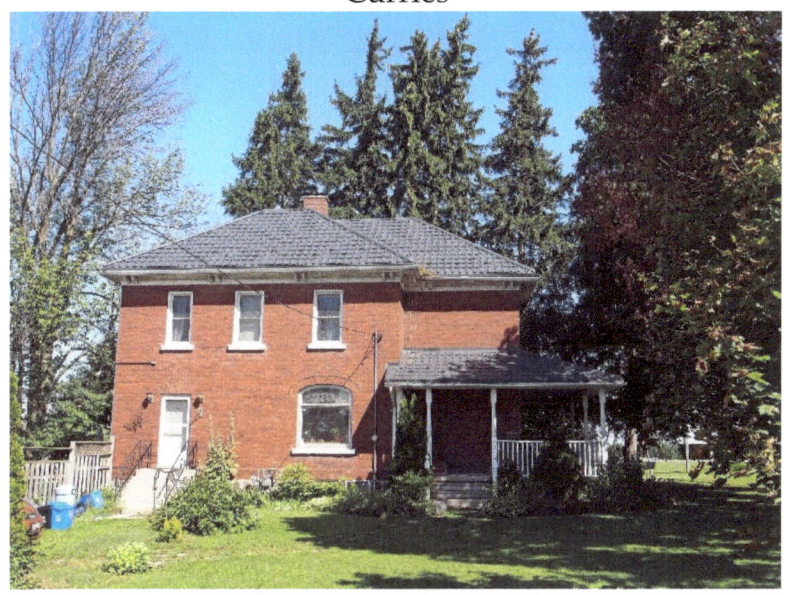

464995 Curries Road

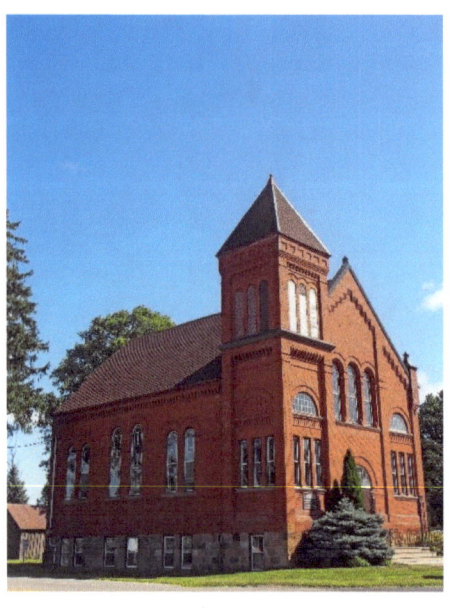

465003 Curries Road - Curries United Church – erected A.D. 1891

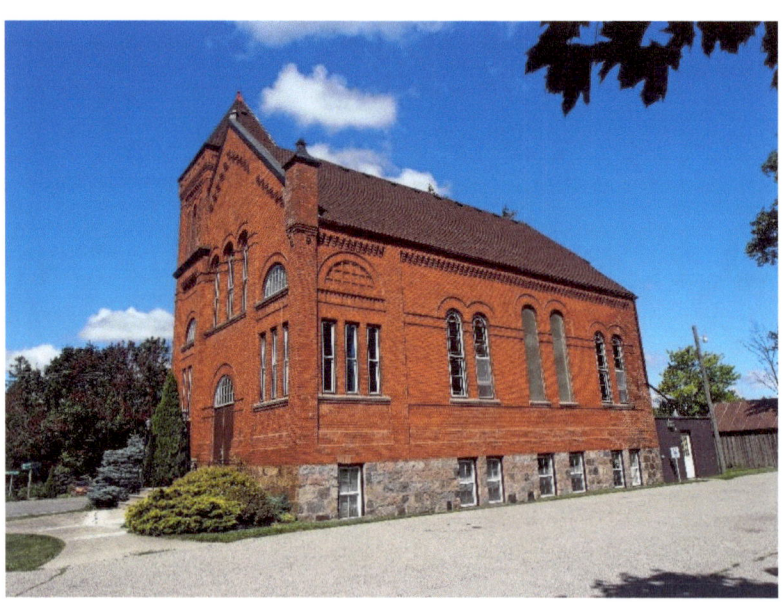

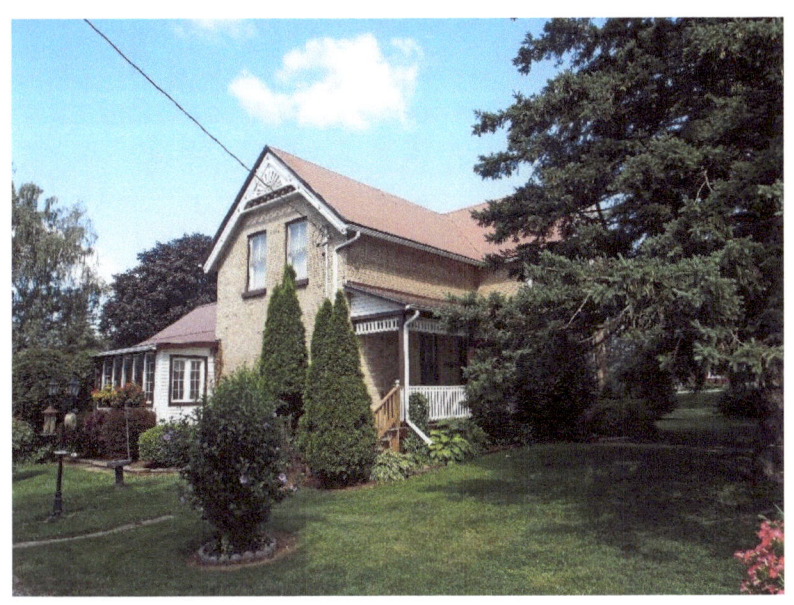

594361 Oxford 59

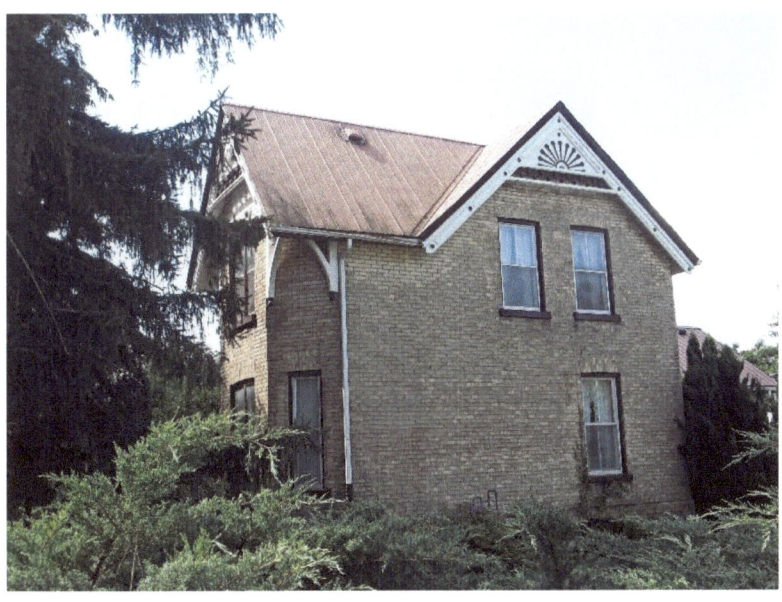

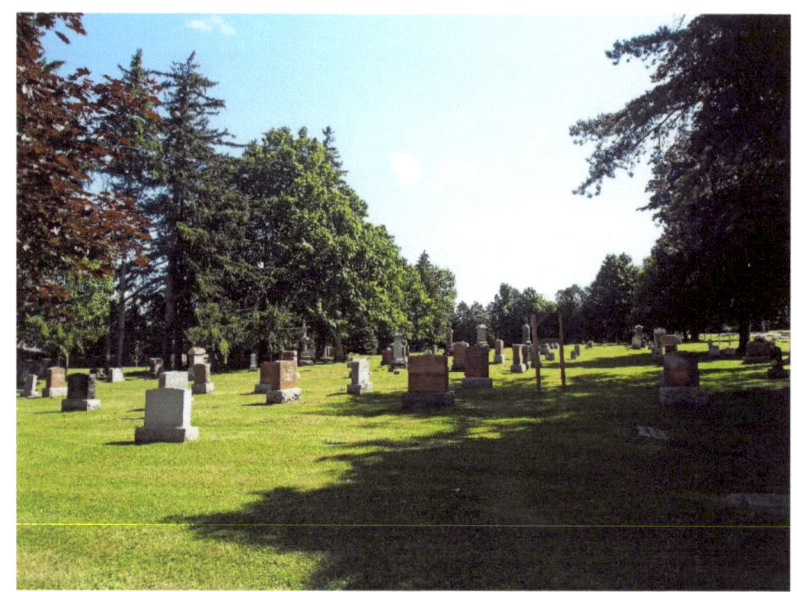
465007 Curries Road – Pleasant View (Curries) Cemetery

Springford

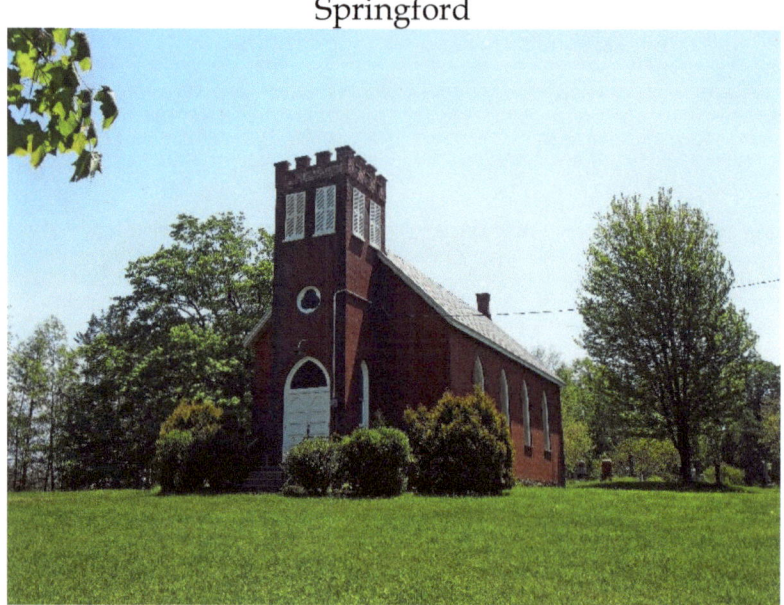
224570 Ostrander Road – St. Charles Anglican Church – 1844

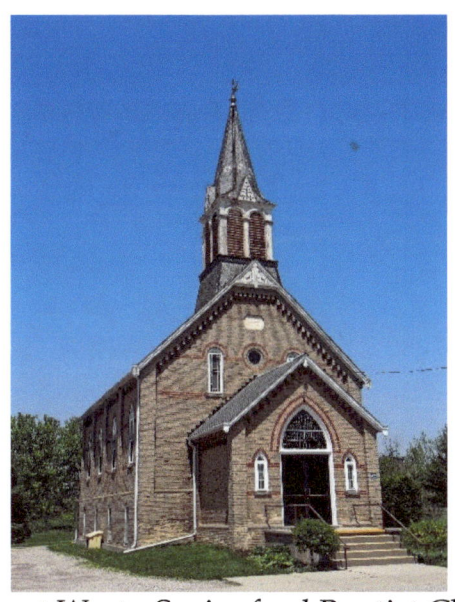

422 Main Street West - Springford Baptist Church – 1887

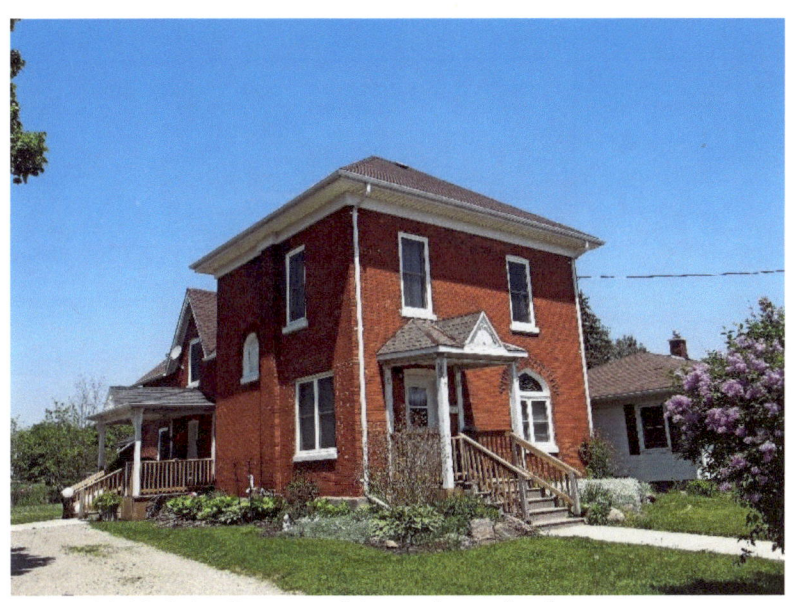

416 Main Street – hipped roof – four-square

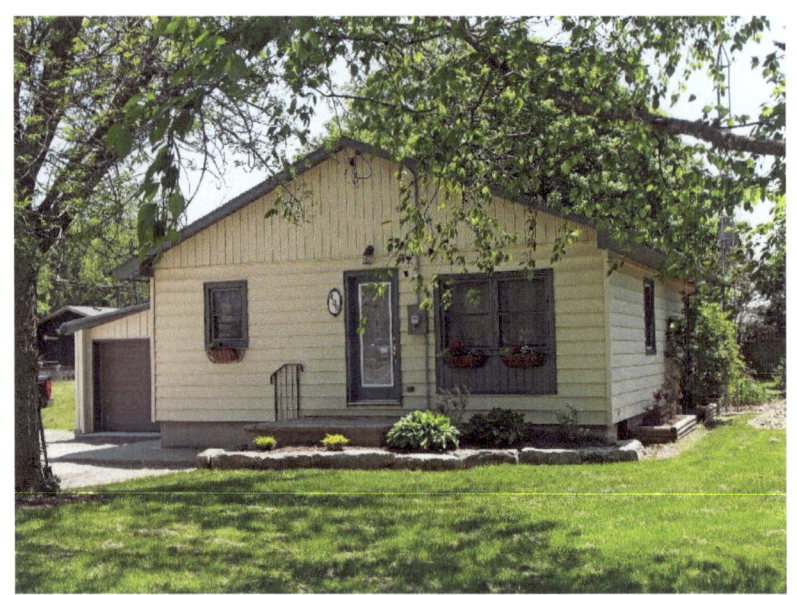

409 Main Street

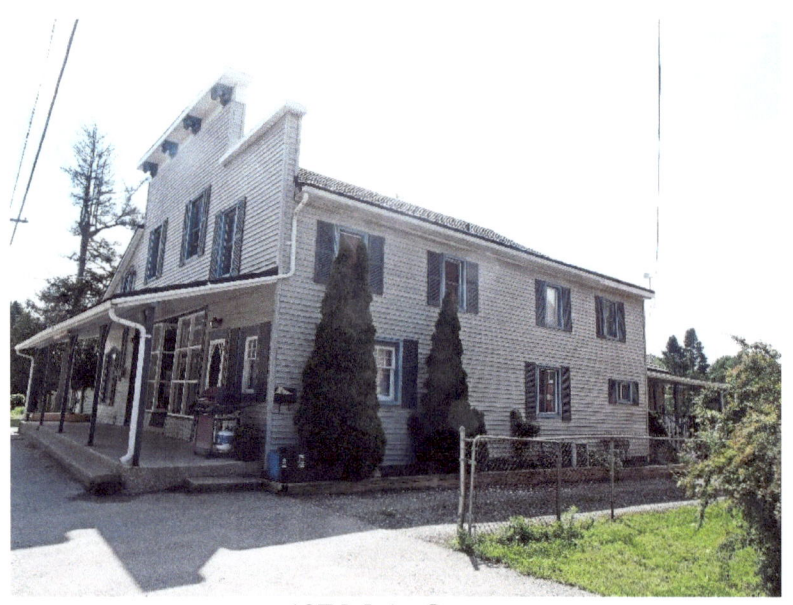

407 Main Street

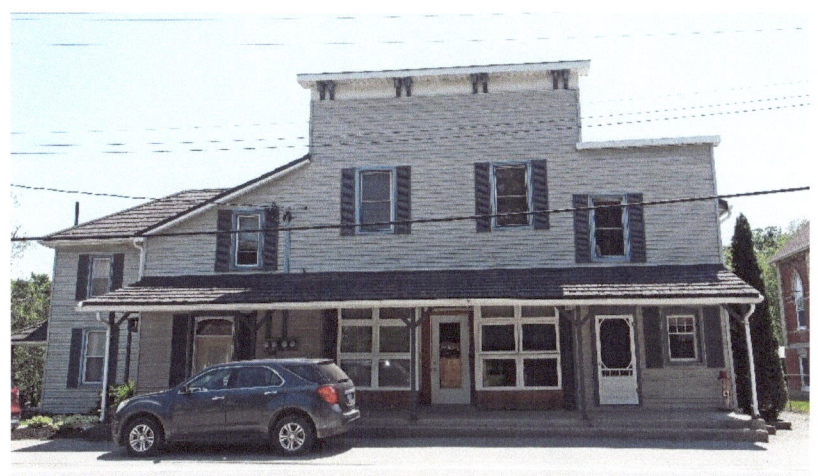

407 Main Street – This early frame store, the centre of the village of Springford, was built in 1850 of post and beam construction with a boom town front. The west wing, also with boom town front, housed the post office from 1852-1977. The first storey façade has two large windows of multi-paned sash, recessed front door and simple porch held by square posts. The east wing of the front façade has a large window with multi-coloured glass in the upper sash.

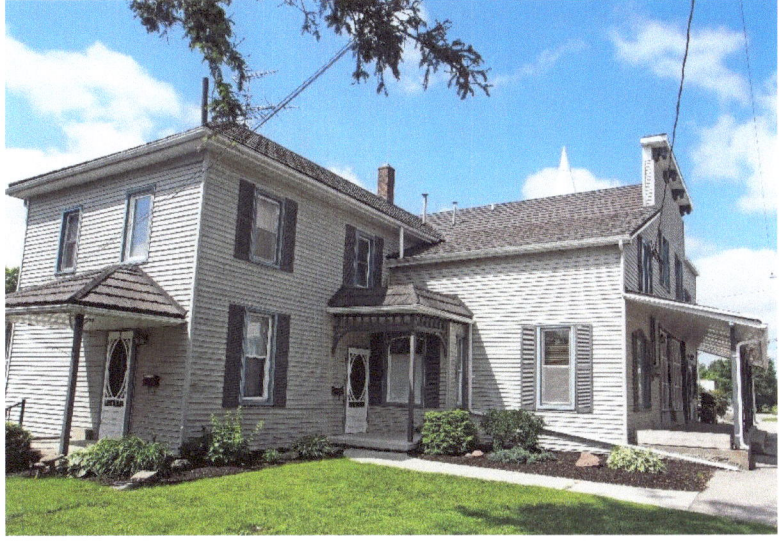

Hipped roof on side extension

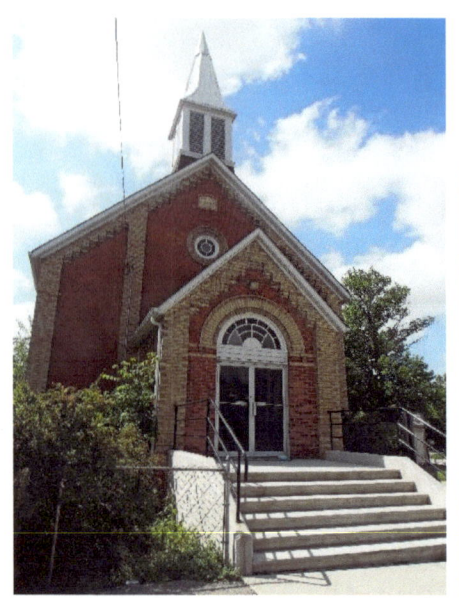
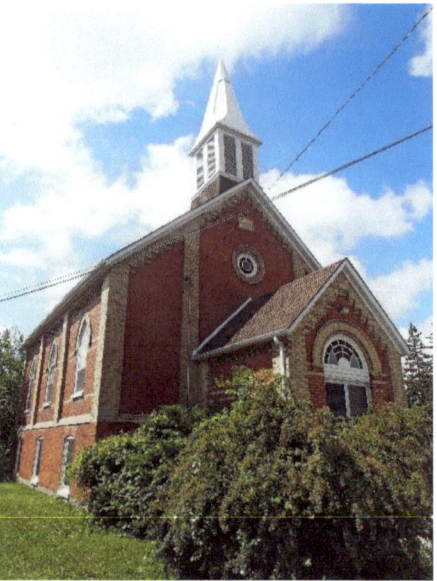

405 Main Street East - Springford United (Sommerfeld Mennonite) Church 1864 – cupola, dichromatic brickwork, banding, dentil molding, lancet windows, rose window, arched multi-paned transom above door

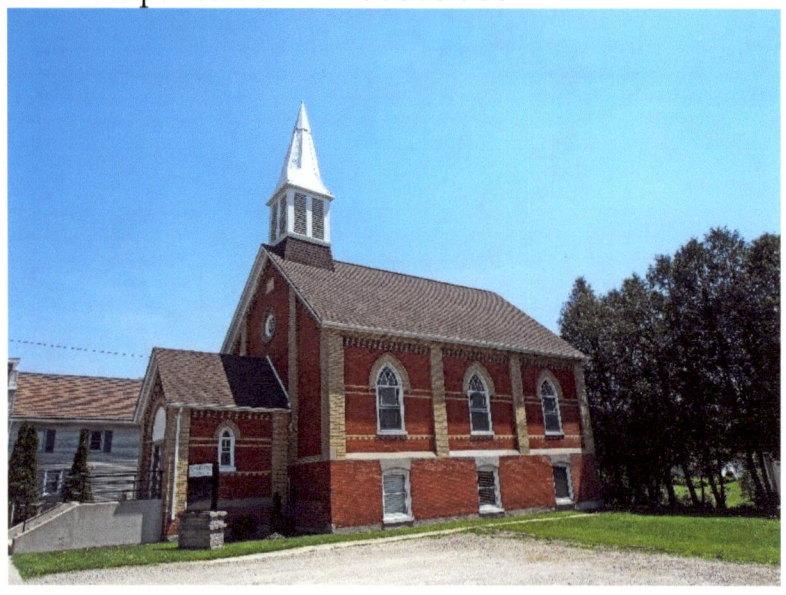

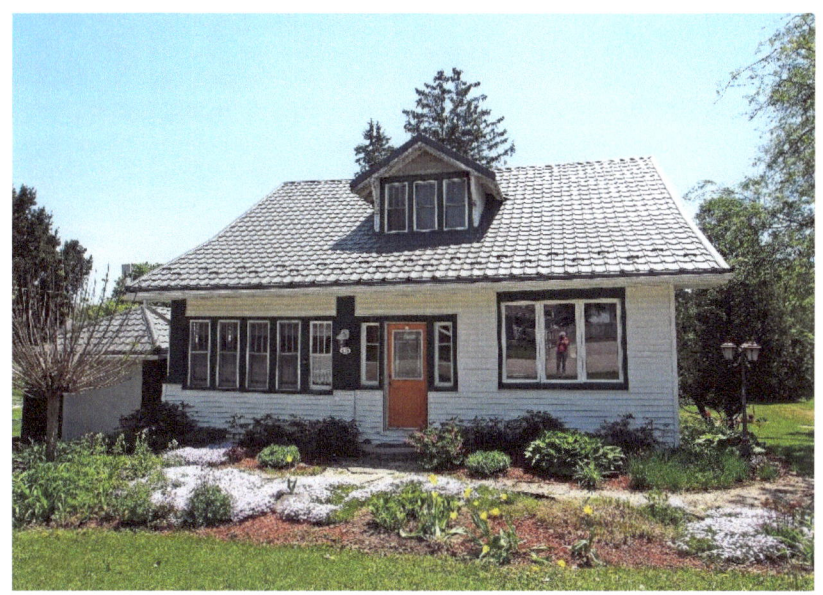

415 Main Street

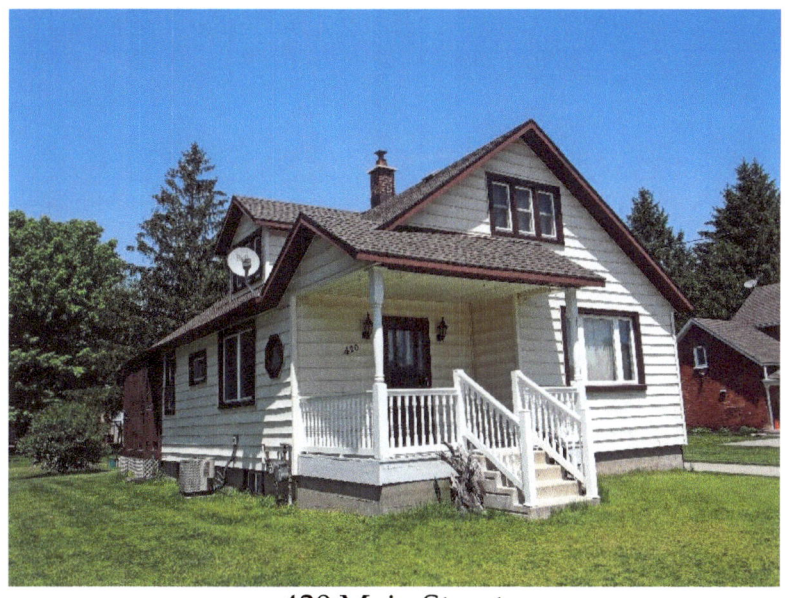

420 Main Street

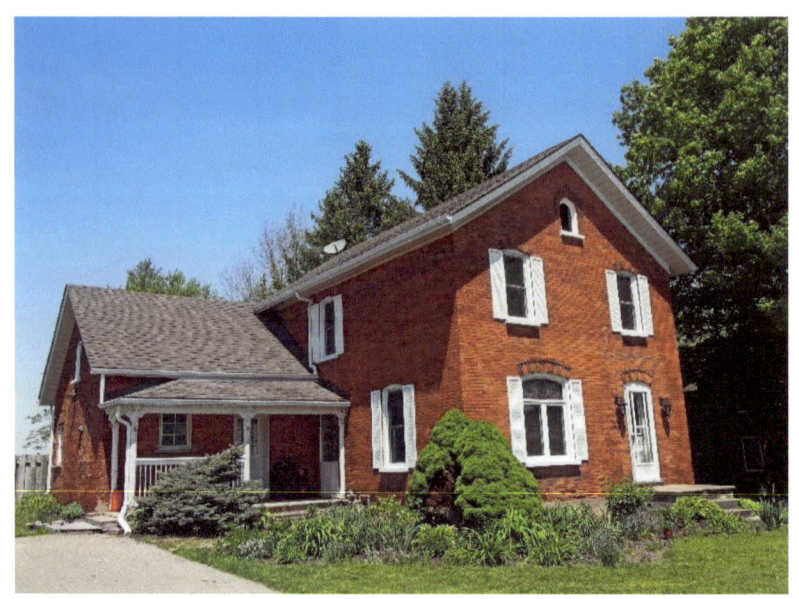

424 Main Street

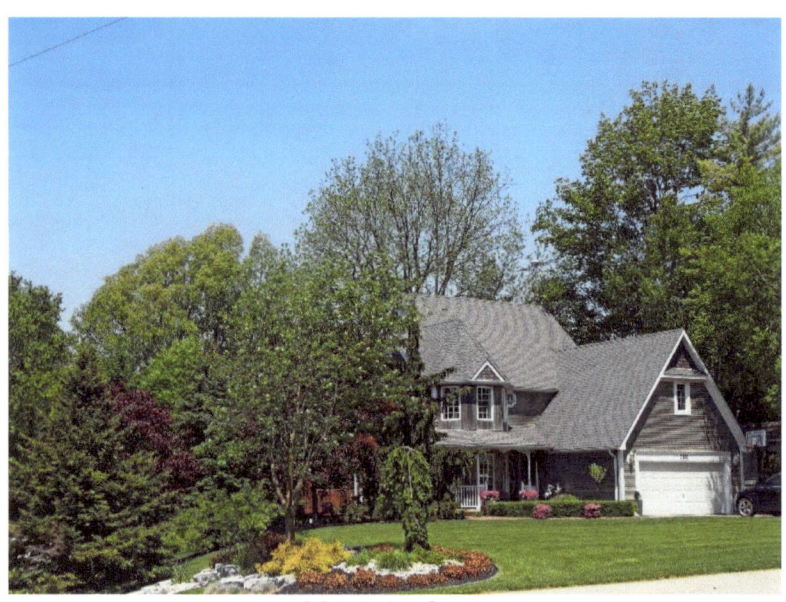

438 Main Street

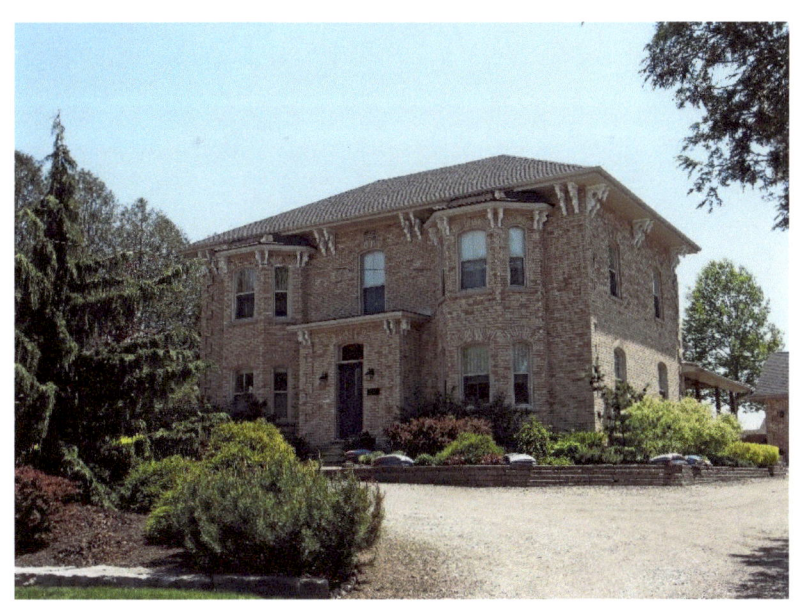

431 Main Street

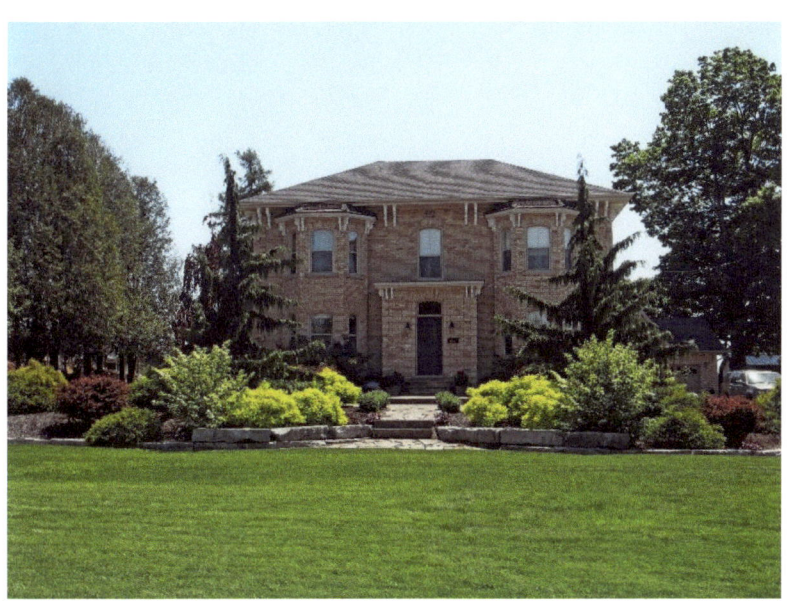

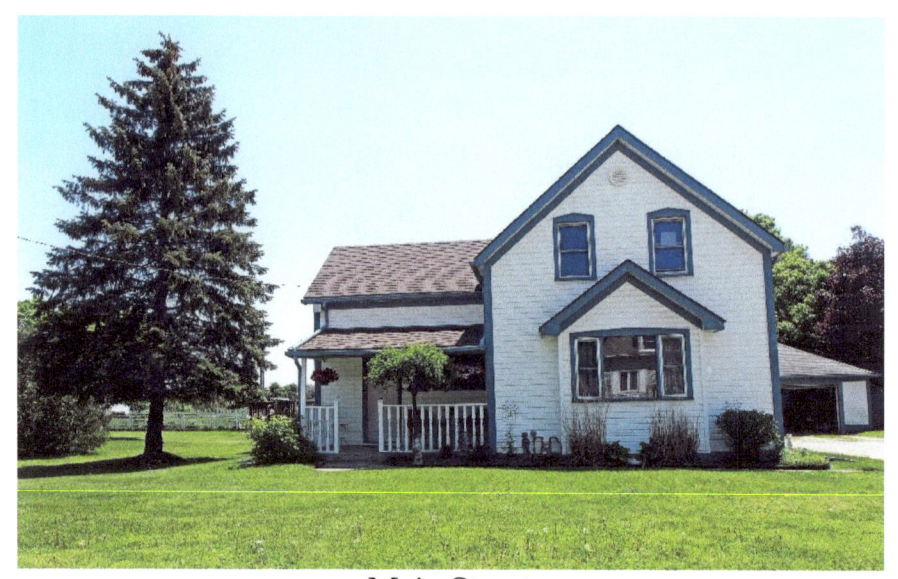

Main Street

Milldale

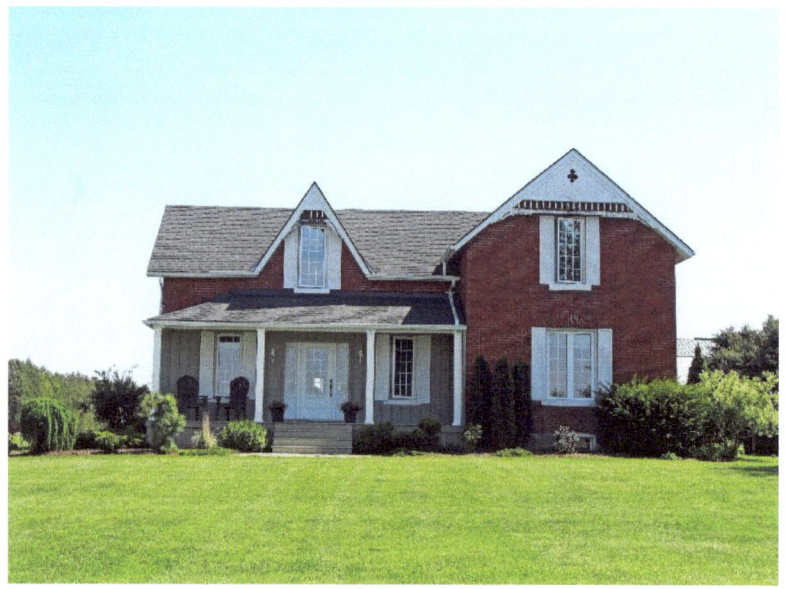

#246080

Other Books by Barbara Raue

Coins of Gold
Arrows, Indians and Love
The Life and Times of Barbara
The Cromwell Family Book
Laura Secord Discovered
Daddy Where Are You?

Montana Series
Book 1: Montana Dream
Book 2: Life on the Montana Frontier
Book 3: Montana to Boston and Back
Book 4: Montana Sons Go to War
Book 5: Montana Sons Return from War

© 2019 by Barbara Raue - All the photos in this book have been taken with my cameras. I own the rights to them.

www.ingramcontent.com/pod-product-compliance
Lightning Source LLC
Chambersburg PA
CBHW040232220526
45473CB00001B/212